DEVELOPMENT CENTRE STUDIES

# AN INSTITUTIONAL
# APPROACH
# TO PROJECT ANALYSIS
## IN DEVELOPING COUNTRIES

by
Olof MURELIUS

Preface by
Göran OHLIN

DEVELOPMENT CENTRE
OF THE ORGANISATION FOR ECONOMIC CO-OPERATION AND DEVELOPMENT

The Organisation for Economic Co-operation and Development (OECD) was set up under a Convention signed in Paris on 14th December 1960, which provides that the OECD shall promote policies designed:

— to achieve the highest sustainable economic growth and employment and a rising standard of living in Member countries, while maintaining financial stability, and thus to contribute to the development of the world economy;

— to contribute to sound economic expansion in Member as well as non-member countries in the process of economic development;

— to contribute to the expansion of world trade on a multilateral, non-discriminatory basis in accordance with international obligations.

The Members of OECD are Australia, Austria, Belgium, Canada, Denmark, Finland, France, the Federal Republic of Germany, Greece, Iceland, Ireland, Italy, Japan, Luxembourg, the Netherlands, New Zealand, Norway, Portugal, Spain, Sweden, Switzerland, Turkey, the United Kingdom and the United States.

*The Development Centre of the Organisation for Economic Co-operation and Development was established by decision of the OECD Council on 23rd October 1962.*

*The purpose of the Centre is to bring together the knowledge and experience available in Member countries of both economic development and the formulation and execution of general policies of economic aid; to adapt such knowledge and experience to the actual needs of countries or regions in the process of development and to put the results at the disposal of the countries by appropriate means.*

*The Centre has a special and autonomous position within the OECD which enables it to enjoy scientific independence in the execution of its task. Nevertheless, the Centre can draw upon the experience and knowledge available in the OECD in the development field.*

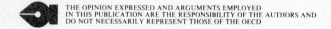

THE OPINION EXPRESSED AND ARGUMENTS EMPLOYED
IN THIS PUBLICATION ARE THE RESPONSIBILITY OF THE AUTHORS AND
DO NOT NECESSARILY REPRESENT THOSE OF THE OECD

Publié en français sous le titre :

LES INSTITUTIONS FACE À
L'ANALYSE DES PROJETS
DANS LES PAYS EN DÉVELOPPEMENT

\*.\*

*Also available*

**MANUAL OF INDUSTRIAL PROJECT ANALYSIS IN DEVELOPING COUN-TRIES.** Methodology and Case Studies (August 1968) Revised edition (February 1972)
(41 68 06 1)   710 pages                                      £4.25    US$12.50    F50.00

**MANAGING INFORMATION FOR RURAL DEVELOPMENT PROJECTS,** by N. Imboden (August 1980)
(41 80 03 1) ISBN 92-64-12039-4   100 pages              £2.90    US$6.50    F26.00

*Prices charged at the OECD Publications Office.*

*THE OECD CATALOGUE OF PUBLICATIONS and supplements will be sent free of charge on request addressed either to OECD Publications Office, 2, rue André-Pascal, 75775 PARIS CEDEX 16, or to the OECD Sales Agent in your country.*

# TABLE OF CONTENTS

CHAPTER V

DEVELOPING PROJECT INSTITUTIONS IN A SOFT SECTOR: RURAL DEVELOPMENT

CHAPTER VI

DEVELOPING DOMESTIC CAPACITY: THE ROLE OF CONSULTANTS

CHAPTER VII

A SUMMING UP

PREFACE

by

Professor Göran Ohlin

The technical literature on the evaluation of investment projects
in developing countries is extensive. Already a decade ago the OECD
Development Centre published the important manual by Little and
Mirrlees. Its methodology, or other similar ones, have by now been
adopted by numerous planning offices, aid agencies and other institutions engaged in development finance.

In this volume, Mr. Murelius examines how project evaluation is
actually carried out, a very different subject. The political and
administrative process by which development projects are designed,
assessed, adopted and implemented is certainly not the same everywhere, but it will always be more of a bureaucratic power game than
an idealized description of the "project cycle" suggests. Mr. Murelius
has spent considerable time in the field to get to know some of the
actors in this game, and he has produced what seems to me a unique
and important study which draws attention to many basic problems in
the organization of planning as a whole.

## Investment and misinvestment

The importance of the subject can hardly be exaggerated. Capital formation is the principal means by which the economic future is shaped,
and the variety of options is enormous. Housing, hospitals, schools,
roads, ports, factories, irrigation systems in different locations
and embodying different technologies are among the potential investments.

It might be tempting to believe that the ideal to which planning
should approach is a ranking of all conceivable projects by their
rate of return so that one could then simply adopt them starting
from the top of the list. In a decentralised economy, one assumes
that individual investors acting under market forces will reach at
least an approximation of such a solution. However, there is always
a need for collective investment in infrastructure or for intervention when social costs are lower or the benefits greater than private ones, e.g. because of the presence of various external factors.
In the public sector, whether it is limited to such needs or covers
much of the economy, as in many developing countries, even a list
limited to projects that might be feasible in view of the general

condition of an economy will simply be too large to make it possible to resort to selection by sifting as a principal tool of planning.

There must be some over-all strategy or conception of development underlying the drawing-up of projects. It is, as Mr. Murelius reminds us, by no means self-evident what a "project" is, but in practice it will be large and complex, and the design phase will be fairly long. This means that by the time a project is ready for appraisal, whether by a national or an external agency, considerable time and effort have already been invested in it, and political and administrative pressures for or against it may be very strong.

If the methods used are so flexible that one can get any result one wants, the project evaluation will be meaningless. Yet there will, of necessity, be margins for dispute and uncertainty. The most meticu-lous appraisal of a long-lived investment project will not be worth more than the assumptions made about such things as future prices. Future benefits may also be weighted differently depending on whom they accrue to, and the rate at which the future is discounted depends on a controversial weighting of the welfare of future gene-rations against that of the present one.

Big projects in the social field will usually not be amenable to meaningful estimates of their social returns, and project appraisal can therefore not help in fine turning of the allocation of re-sources between different sectors. But it remains essential as a way to prevent gross waste. What project appraisal can do- apart from checking technical assumptions and such important things as gestation periods and running-in time- is to correct the optical illusions which arise when the costs and benefits of a project are assessed in prices that do not express the social cost of the resources to be used or the value of the output expected.

The price system is distorted by taxes, subsidies, monopolistic positions and exchange control, and the social cost of employing unutilised resources is lower than their cost in the market. It is only too easy, therefore, to arrive at the impression that a project is eminently profitable although a careful analysis would show that even if all works out as predicted the project will be a drain on the economy instead of contributing to it. That this is no remote risk has been shown by costly experience.

Apart from sabotaging growth, such misinvestment may also produce debt servicing difficulties if funds are borrowed abroad. The magni-tudes involved, if billions of dollars are invested at negative rates of return, make it more than warranted to be vigilant.

## External pressure

Most of the initiatives for systematic appraisal of development projects have come from aid donors or other financial agencies. Although
public funds are not allocated for domestic investments in industrialised countries without careful investigation, there is little doubt
that foreign aid projects have been subjected to far more intensive
scrutiny. A major reason for this has undoubtedly been lack of confidence that the political system and administrative machinery in
developing countries would ensure appropriate use of the money. Lending agencies also have a need to convince themselves that they have
a good chance of being repaid.

Whether or not such objectives are met by project evaluation is not
so clear. As is often pointed out, the net effect of making finance
available for a good project may be that the borrowing country is
free to spend resources in an entirely different field, and future
debt servicing capacity will hinge more on general management and
balance-of-payments performance than on individual projects.

Although scrutiny by external agencies is often felt to be irksome,
it will be useful if it makes it easier to perform the screening
function referred to above. However, outside agencies are not always
presented with a ready-made project for approval or rejection. They
are often involved in the project preparation at an earlier stage,
and if an appraisal threatens to be unfavorable there may well be
changes in the project design- or of the premises on which it is
appraised- rather than outright rejection.

However, the mere fact that two bureaucracies, and sometimes more,
with different organisational principles, terminologies and resources
are involved makes it inevitable that the process becomes even more
cumbersome and slow.

The standing complaint from loan officers and planners in developing
countries has been that the shadow-pricing techniques recommended
to them for social cost-benefit analysis are too complicated, especially for application in countries with modest planning capacity.

Not only in this context but in all phases of the project cycle,
international consulting firms have come to play a prominent role,
and Mr. Murelius draws welcome attention to this important subject.
It is sometimes assumed that consultants can meet any deficiencies
of experience or management skills. No matter how useful the services
they contribute and how indispensable they are, they do constitute
yet another set of actors and make the process even more full of
potential friction.

## The project shortage

One merit of Mr. Murelius's work is to make it clear that project appraisal cannot be approached in isolation from the whole project cycle and especially from product design. The most telling evidence of the importance of his subject matter is the paradox that in spite of the evident investment needs in developing countries, financing agencies complain about the dearth of projects.

Many countries have built up an admirable capacity for planning and have also become less dependent on concessional aid as they have been able to turn to the private market for finance. But the hard core of world poverty remains, and the least developed countries will depend on aid for a long time yet. They need sizeable projects in irrigation, transportation, and many other areas, and they are ill equipped to produce them. "Preinvestment aid is in short supply". One may hope that technical cooperation among developing countries will become increasingly helpful in this context.

Mr. Murelius's analysis has not only led him to some suggestions for improvement, it also constitutes a useful guide on how to avoid mistakes. If some of his conclusions do not seem to apply to conditions in countries he did not have an opportunity to study or are disputed because other interpretations are proposed, his study will still have served to initiate an important inquiry.

Professor Göran Ohlin

University of Uppsala, 1980.

# CHAPTER I

INTRODUCTION: INSTITUTIONS, PROJECTS AND AID

This study examines various institutional aspects of the manner in which projects in developing countries supported by aid agencies are identified, financed and appraised. It argues that adequate domestic capacity for policy analysis, resource allocation, project selection and management is indispensable, yet donors, lenders and recipients have not always succeeded in building the required institutions and systems. This is partly because the issue has been regarded as too sensitive and partly because its long-run importance has not been recognised.

It is further argued that this is a major reason for the mutual disenchantment with aid, as witnessed by the discomfort experienced by many over the Basic Needs Strategy, and for the doubts that proposals for a Massive Transfer of Resources (MTR) or a New International Economic Order (NIEO) can be translated into action. There has been a considerable increase in project assistance to developing countries, especially through multilateral agencies such as the World Bank, with special emphasis on such sectors as rural development and basic health care. Growing project volume and sectors with complex project design underline the need for increased domestic capacity as well as changes in external criteria. At present the cost of project-analysis methods and procedures introduced from outside is likely to be greater than the corresponding benefit because sufficient practical attention is not given to related institution-building.

The situation is serious: as the decade of the 1980s begins, aid weariness has passed into a stage of quiet crisis. Aid is not the issue it used to be when it was believed that a level of 1 per cent of GNP would make a significant difference, and in particular when there was hope for a 2 per cent level once the original commitment was fulfilled. Estimates within the World Bank suggest that the average level of aid will at best reach 0.35 per cent in the mid-1980s.

In the industrialised countries disbelief in development assistance is spreading as a consequence of their own reduced growth and a lack of evidence of the effectiveness of aid except as humanitarian relief. Aid is increasingly used as an instrument for export promotion, and in practice it can become a form of concealed protectionism. Under present world economic conditions it is no longer difficult for a donor country to justify increased tying of aid: obligations at home are pressing, and for the recipient tied aid is presumed to be better than none.

In the developing countries aid is increasingly regarded as a substitute, however important, for changes in the international system which could provide a sufficient condition for development. Domestic problems - poverty, regional imbalance and inequality - are recognised, and the threat of internal conflict caused by unstable modern and traditional sectors is a constant reality. It appears that the problems of development cooperation can only be resolved by institutional changes on both sides. We therefore examine the nature of various related institutions and their ability to cope with increased volume, changes in sectoral allocation and demands for improved effectiveness. We are looking not primarily at manpower, including training, attitudes, incentives, management and coordination, but at the policies which influence the environment in which institutions and manpower operate.

We hope to show that aid could become an instrument to promote North-South accommodation by improving recipients' absorptive capacity and by making donors' procedures more effective. This would require a reorganisation and decentralisation of aid with a view to speeding up the transfer of resources, encouraging relations based on mutual interest, and stimulating increased mutual commitment.

In the case of Swedish aid, some of this has occurred already and the experiences of SIDA will be examined at several points in this study. There has been considerable debate over the years regarding the composition and effectiveness of the Swedish aid programme, the justification of projects and programmes and the merits of individual recipients. Two overrriding concerns have been the increase in volume up to the 1 per cent level and respect for priorities established by the recipient. It is accepted by Sweden that it should be a "concerned participant" in the development effort of its programme countries, but as a general rule the priorities of the recipient are accepted so long as they do not conflict with the fundamental objectives of Swedish development assistance. This has created a sense of mutual trust and facilitated some innovations.

A recent note on Swedish aid policy describes some salient features of Swedish development assistance which illustrate the contradictions and conflicts inherent in the aid effort. It is recognised that basic needs-oriented activities increase problems of absorptive capacity.

Growing experience of the difficulties involved in trying to reach
the poorest strata of the population has therefore prompted development of more flexible aid procedures. Also important in this respect
have been the rapid increase in appropriations and efforts to avoid
unspent balances. Flexible procedures were facilitated by certain
constitutional and political factors:

- Strong public support for aid. The target of 1 per cent of GNP
  was reached in the fiscal year 1975/76 after a series of annual
  increases of 25 per cent. This has made it possible and necessary for the Government to be less stringent as far as controls
  are concerned.

- Government authority to commit aid funds on a three-year basis.
  Only very large investment projects have to be submitted for
  parliamentary approval.

- An independent aid agency (SIDA), responsible to the Government
  as a whole and not to a single ministry, which takes decisions
  on aid content.

- Considerable authority delegated to field offices, which can,
  for example, allocate funds among different activities or prolong
  agreements on specific activities.

The rate of disbursements increased considerably with the new flexibility permitted by the Parliament and Government; project assistance
decreased while sectoral assistance and budget and import support
increased. This has been a consequence of the move away from rigorous appraisal of individual activities and stringent legal and
accounting requirements. SIDA admits, however, that the aid programme has suffered qualitatively, since its ability to "engage in the
preparation of projects and programmes of a more complicated nature
has not been commensurate with resource availability". On the other
hand, it believes that the choice of programme countries has been
"comparatively positive", maintaining that in principle aid funds
should be considered and dealt with as "ordinary government income...
subject only to the rules and regulations of the recipient". However,
in practice some recipients demand "concerned participation", and
the Swedish Parliament and auditing authorities require "a reasonable rendering of accounts". These requirements have been difficult
to satisfy. Nevertheless, by international standards there has been
little parliamentary or public criticism with regard to accounting,
follow-up, and evaluation applied to the Swedish aid programme.

The evolution of Swedish aid management highlights the issues of
this study. Conventional project aid, where funds are applied to a
defined input in the expectation of a predicted output, is often

tied to external criteria (use of technology, appraisal methodology); though this is supported in donor countries, it can cause resentment in recipient countries. There must be mutual accommodation if project aid is to survive and meet new priorities. Recipients prefer a more fluid situation with funds available for less specific purposes, but this is seldom acceptable to donors. Both approaches to aid (project vs. sectoral assistance and budget support) require mutual improvements in the "processing" of aid. The considerable uncertainty in developing countries over investments and their impact means that "learning by doing" should be permitted. However, this cannot be freely admitted by donors and recipients to their constituencies, since it involves considerable risk.

## I. Project Financing and the Project Cycle (1)

It is not necessary in the context of this study to deal in detail with all aspects of project financing and the project cycle. Our emphasis will be on project selection (identification, preparation and appraisal) but we shall also show how important problems of implementation and evaluation are for project selection.

The components of project financing can be best described in terms of the project cycle which, following the World Bank's convention, can be divided into six stages: identification, preparation, appraisal, negotiation, implementation/supervision and evaluation. Ideally, each stage of the cycle should proceed as follows:

At the identification stage, both the donor/lender and recipient/ borrower are engaged to varying degrees in bringing forward project ideas for consideration. The capacity of the recipient/borrower determines the extent to which both parties are involved. Projects have to correspond to what both wish to have funded. Sometimes projects are identified exclusively by the donor/lender during surveys or by private interests in the country.

During the preparation stage, close cooperation between the recipient/ borrower and the donor/lender is desirable, especially if domestic capacity is weak. All aspects of project design, including the techniques to be used and the administrative institutions, should be taken care of at this stage.

Project appraisal can be done by both parties either separately or together. The donor/lender is usually closely involved to make sure that the project is viable. Technical appraisal deals with the appropriateness of techniques and how best to procure them; institutional appraisal involves organisation and administration; economic analysis includes cost-benefit analysis related to national and sectoral objectives; financial analysis establishes the sources of funds and

their scheduling, the relation between costs and benefits, the rate
of return to the enterprise, and often the payback period and the
break-even point.

At the negotiation stage, the agreed measures of the project are
turned into legal obligations.

During implementation the parties concerned supervise execution and
the disbursement of funds. At this stage all the various problems
and risks become apparent, and technical assistance by the donor/
lender can be of great value.

The aim of evaluation, which is seldom carried out in detail by
either the donor/lender or the recepient/borrower, is to compare the
actual outcome of the project with projections made in the appraisal.
An examination of the essential positive and negative effects of the
project can provide important lessons for future preparation and
identification.

This general view of the project cycle is presented as background to
subsequent chapters in which we analyse the roles of different interests.

## II. Six Questions about Project-Initiating Institutions

During the course of this study, we shall address ourselves to six
major questions:

1. To what extent have project-appraisal techniques been adopted
   by administrative units in developing countries, given the
   pressure to use them as a way to ensure a more efficient use
   of aid?

2. To what extent do factors other than decision-making techniques,
   notably political tying of aid and the dictates of the international commodity, capital and technology markets, prede-
   termine the outcome of investment appraisals?

3. In which ways do project-selection methods influence the development of the institutions where they are applied?

4. Does the present emphasis on poverty require development of
   new types of institutions, and how far should project-selection
   criteria be adapted to meet the multiple goals of rural development? In view of the aims of rural development to reach particular target groups, should a single-project institution encompass all aspects of the project cycle?

5. How can external manpower, in the form of consultants, best be
   used to develop domestic institutions?

6. Finally, can external assistance be used to strengthen these institutions and hence project selection, and what form might this take?

This study is an effort to fill a gap: how "things get done" is universally recognised to be of great importance, but in books and manuals on project selection, financing and resource allocation, this is usually glossed over. Such realities can seldom be quantified, and they are therefore usually relegated to comments about the "human factor". Comparisons and inferences are difficult because of the great past and present variations between individuals, institutions, and countries. Publications on project selection methods (2) say little about economic and social institutions although many recognise their importance, and some have emphasized the limitations of economic and financial analysis.

Robert Chambers sums it up this way: "There is a profound conditioning of those who have been through the process of being trained in cost-benefit analysis, and indeed of becoming economists, into supposing that finance is the scarcest resource to which others should be reduced. In practice, when you come to the implementation of projects the scarcest resource is often found to be what one might call administrative capacity, or the capacity to get things done" (3).

We shall not elaborate on the usefulness of cost-benefit analysis and other forms of project appraisal but will make observations as appropriate (4). A number of important texts have appeared which provide a more general treatment of project financing (5), but they contain no comprehensive treatment of institutional aspects.

However, some books and journals have emphasised the importance of project management and administration (6) and the interdependence of appraisal and evaluation (7). Rondinelli (8) has described the impact of the "imperious rationality" of development assistance policy on project administration as follows: "Perhaps the ultimate irony is that many developing countries have been judged backward, inefficient, and defective in public planning and administration because they cannot apply analytical and management systems techniques, the efficiency and practicality of which remain unproven even in advanced industrialised nations".

He suggests that if projects are to produce institutional and economic development,"change must be internally generated and intimately related to national, political, cultural and organisational needs and constraints... Ultimately the most effective methods of project planning and management are those that improve decision-making capacities of national officials within their own policy-making systems".

III. The Scope of this Study

Much has been written about how things "ought to be done", and the
fact that they are not done "properly" is ascribed to administrative
constraints. The usual prescription is that political systems and
administrative structures be "improved". In this study we describe
how things have been done and extrapolate suggestions for institutional change and administrative improvements.

The study is based on experience gained by the author with the
Swedish International Development Authority (SIDA) and during his
secondment in 1973-76 to the Development Centre of OECD for work on
project analysis in developing countries. During this time he visited
Brazil, Colombia, Costa Rica, Indonesia, Nigeria, Peru, Philippines,
Tanzania and Thailand, where he collected project submission formats,
guidelines, manuals and similar material. He held discussions with
staff members of ministries, state agencies, banks, consultancy firms,
aid agencies and development institutions. The empirical basis of the
study is a comparative analysis of different countries and multilateral agencies carried out in 1976 with information gathered between
1974-1976. It is believed that the conclusions derived from this
analysis, together with subsequent events and observations of development co-operation, make them as relevant now as a few years ago.

Chapter II contains a brief discussion of various appraisal techniques (such as cost-benefit analysis) that have been proposed, particularly by multilateral agencies, and the degree of dependence of
developing countries on Western technology, finance and commodities.
These external interests often distort resource allocation because
of their concern with growth or equitable income distribution.
Domestic interests are also discussed, and we show that power and
expertise have tended to concentrate in some sectors and not in others,
which we believe is a major determinant of fund allocation, particularly for funds from multilateral and bilateral donors and lenders.
This is analysed in the context of "hard" sectors (physical infrastructure, industry) and "soft" sectors (health, education, rural
development). These various aspects are considered in relation to
the development of indigenous institutions.

Chapter III describes the project-selection process in five developing countries: Brazil, Nigeria, Peru, Tanzania and Thailand. The
size, structure and nature of the institutions that carry out project
selection are discussed, as well as the methods used and the social
and economic context in which they operate. National objectives are
examined in relation to project-investment criteria. Observations
are made on the relative success or failure of certain institutions.

Investments cannot be considered in isolation from the requirements and objectives of external interests, notably suppliers of capital, equipment and experts. In Chapter IV we describe the role of bilateral and selected multilateral agencies (the World Bank, the United Nations Development Programme and the Inter-American Development Bank) and their influence on project selection.

In Chapter V we look at rural development planning, a "soft" sector with multiple objectives, specific target groups, great uncertainty of impact compared with "hard" sectors and pressure to expand investment. We briefly discuss the relevance of cost-benefit and cost-effectiveness analyses to this sector. We try to determine whether institutions should accommodate external demands for project appraisal or whether new criteria and appraisal techniques could be evolved to fit domestic institutions and forms of rural financing.

A matter central to the entire study - the role of external consultants - is discussed in Chapter VI. In particular, we see how consultants could be used to strengthen domestic institutions instead of being confined to short-term assignments. In this context, it is surprising but understandable that accounting and audit are overlooked in development cooperation. Surprising because policy and programming should be predicated on some estimate and verification of the costs and benefits of alternative activities, as well as their wider implications. Understandable because accounting is an instrument for determining the accountability of the principal actors and institutions. Accounting is indispensible for the wise allocation and effective use of scarce resources and will most likely be recognised by decision-makers as such in the years to come.

In the last chapter, we offer some answers to the questions raised about project-initiating institutions and discuss policy implications for improving them, in particular through new forms of development assistance.

CHAPTER II


GENERAL ISSUES IN PROJECT ANALYSIS

I. DEPENDENCE ON METHODOLOGY, FINANCE AND TECHNOLOGY

Over the last 30 years the pattern of economic development in less developed countries (LDCs) and the allocation of financial aid by rich nations has brought about the growth of techniques in project analysis, i.e. the identification and selection of projects by pre-selected criteria. These techniques are usually based on the efficiency criterion (maximising the ratio of benefits, in the form of increments to GNP, to costs) although efforts have been made, in response to political pressures, to diversify them to include sectors not normally amenable to straightforward net-benefit maximisation approaches and to include, apart from efficiency, other criterion such as equity.

A number of agencies have produced methodologies of project appraisal over the last ten years. These agencies include OECD (1), UNIDO (2), the World Bank (3), the British ODA (4), and the USAID (5).

It is not necessary here to enter the debate on the relative merits of each technique; there is a huge literature on the subject. In practice the techniques are not widely applied at present, except under pressure from external donors. A major problem is that the techniques, which have been developed in multilateral and bilateral donor agencies by academics are far too complicated, time-consuming and expensive to be adopted in their entirety by institutions in developing countries.

Appraisal criteria used and recommended by various external agencies place restricting burdens on recipients. The following summary indicates this burden; as the basic principle of project appraisal is an effort to establish commercial or national profitability, what is required are: a) the identification of the quantity, quality and timing of inputs and outputs, b) estimation of the values of those inputs and outputs in order to compute the costs and benefits, and c) comparison of these costs and benefits with each other and with those of alternative projects compared in a similarly consistent manner.

The principle is simple, but the application is never easy. We shall discuss later the demands made on agencies to derive shadow prices and will only point here to the difficulty of making the right assumption and assigning correct values to costs and benefits. Often quantification is near impossible, especially for benefits.

Obviously good project design is expensive, although so is bad project selection. It has been stated repeatedly that the lack of well prepared projects is a basic constraint on development, but pressure for implementation tends to postpone the establishment of the required infrastructure for project planning.

Project identification must emanate and draw from sector analysis. This is particularly true in sectors such as transport, power, telecommunications and education.

Another problem is that methods of project analysis must be part of a system of decision-making that confirms its value. Many developing countries have established offices of project evaluation in the planning agency with formal authority to screen projects. Nevertheless projects often bypass them. In several countries it appears that about half the projects were approved without the planning agency's concurrence. The head of one planning agency explained that while Western management methods were a great contribution, in his country "problem-solving was not done by a straight line" and suggested that somebody ought to spend more time there to study the decision-making process.

Although some 90 % of development financing comes from domestic resources, developing countries are heavily dependent on other forms of external inputs. For example, while the financial contribution of foreign investments in Latin America during 1950-60 was less than 5 % of capital formation, technological inputs from abroad often amounted to 50 % and more, especially in the modern sector (6).

This dependence on foreign technology is in direct conflict with the efforts of LDCs to meet rather ambitious development targets (7), which would require less dependence on manufactured imports, more exports of locally manufactured products and substantially more financial assistance.

Today 90 % of the world's technologists and scientists are active in the industrially advanced countries, and their work is almost exclusively concentrated on already developed markets. Their findings are largely converted into protected technical processes, and international patent law ensures that the knowledge required by the less developed countries can be obtained from foreign private enterprises (8).

This background is an important part of the framework within which developing countries must establish their objectives and priorities and select, design and execute their investment projects.

Dependence on Western finance can be observed in planning agencies where external agencies insist upon budgetary processes and criteria for project analysis. Developing countries usually feel ambivalent about this; they find these constraints excessive although they recognise the need for greater domestic capacity and improvements in the system.

Structural changes repeatedly recommended as a precondition for progress are not likely to be established without substantial assistance and concessions from the industrially advanced countries. To a considerable extent planning in developing countries at national, sector and project levels must follow the constraints of the international capital, commodity and technology markets. As long as the planning of major investment projects is done by outside experts and consultants, there will also be inadequate incentive to train domestic staff. Dependence on funds that require extensive appraisal investigations leads to a dependence on consultants. A multilateral funding agency such as the World Bank depends on them heavily; within the UNDP it is recognised that results are obtained faster through their use, which may save a year or two in implementation, an important factor during periods of rapid inflation and currency deterioration. Some UN Specialised Agencies tend to resist the use of external consultants, since individual experts are easier to handle and consultants as a rule do not transfer enough knowledge. Consultants used by bilateral agencies are normally part of the tying of aid.

## II. PLANNING, POWER AND DOMESTIC INTERESTS

It is easy to overlook the progress which has been made by LDCs in the field of planning, for inadequacies are still serious. Planning systems in most developing countries have been in operation in one form or another for some time; in many countries, planning still takes place under duress because of the insufficient strength of domestic administration and staff resources.

The origin of planning in developing countries was often connected with external demands related to financial and technical assistance, and this influence is still considerable. Early planning thus had a bias which tended to increase dependence. The imprint on planning came from market economies with a great competitive advantage at the international level. Even if it was argued that planning of public activities was indispensible to sound decision-making and financial stability, an objective of early plans was to facilitate integration with the international economy.

Another factor influencing early planning was the recognition by domestic vested interests that planning was intended to promote change which would challenge their positions and privileges (9). Planning was by definition an enemy of status quo and thus a problem of power rather than of techniques and administration. Planners in mixed-economy developing countries discovered that the response of the private sector largely determined the success of the plans and that power relations within and between departments and agencies could easily be upset by allocations proposed by the planning agency.

There has been an extensive debate on planning. Albert Waterston noted over a decade ago, that "where a country's government is reasonably stable and its political leaders give high priority to development, a country generally develops even when there is no formal plan" (10).

Others have suggested that planning is a facade (11) hiding intense bargaining (12), and reflecting "concessions that have had to be made to certain power centres" (13).

There has always been a "crisis" in planning, and it is likely to continue for this is in its nature. On the one hand, national planning has largely been the prerogative of macro-economists with limited interest in projects, and concrete plans, which require a good deal of project planning, have been neglected. On the other hand, where planning has been done at project level, it has generally disregarded the fact that market prices often are misleading (14).

Under any circumstances political and administrative power tends to negate the division between analysis and decision-making. As a rule planners approve or reject projects on the basis of tacit or explicit dictates by those in power, and the definition and quantification of costs and benefits is the "professional" way of doing it.

Historically, planning was superimposed from above and administratively separated from operational responsibility. Since objectives, policy and measures are inseparable, a method should be found to diffuse the discipline of planning throughout the entire administrative system (15).

Diffusion of power within the planning community can now be seen in the trend towards decentralisation and participatory planning, which may be irreversible. This raises questions of efficiency; budgetary planning and management at regional and local levels must be strict and well communicated, and much conventional planning must remain at the central level.

Political decisions to decentralise have been tried, and the results which have been evaluated suggest that systems analysis and administrative design are important. For example, the establishment of local development committees and related block grants in Eastern Africa has been studied by Chambers. He points out that during the first two years the development committees in Kenya failed to put down roots, and that: "a prior condition for the effective working of the committees was a capability higher in the government machine to set guidelines and make requests for action which the government machine could then handle. Such a capability takes time to develop" (16).

In most countries, the author concludes, the best system appears to consist of: "larger policy-oriented development committees of politicians and civil servants; and smaller action-oriented executive committees mainly or entirely of civil servants" (17).

In such a situation, in Chambers' opinion, block grants are valuable as a means to encourage local participation and appropriate project selection and design, thereby improving the way in which decisions are made.

The role of power within domestic agencies is an important determinant of project selection and hence fund disbursement. All potential projects have their vested interests and, although turning down an unsound project will favour development, it is likely to alienate a powerful interest group. Good project analysis requires the expression of unpopular views, but there is little incentive for a member of staff to become a devil's advocate. Even where the effective powers are just and administration is rational, staff members tend to avoid making trouble. Domestic structures of this kind are reinforced by external pressures.

As we have already indicated, the tool of cost-benefit analysis can be abused by vested interests. The considerable uncertainty in predicting socio-economic effects that exists in developing countries, in addition to a scanty data base coupled with a large number of assumptions inherent in the technique, means that the worth of a project can be calculated to suit any interested party. Where cost-benefit analysis is relied upon for deciding between projects, it tends to be in sectors where quantification is easy. Much rests on the successful estimation of benefits. In a less developed country uncertainty is greater than in developed countries.

Hirschman has compared a project in such a country to "a long voyage of discovery in the most varied domains, from technology to politics" (18). In discussing project selection under uncertainty, he elaborates on what he calls the principle of the "Hiding Hand" (19).

Difficulties are beneficially hidden for us so that the required creativity can be mobilized and put to use. In other words, we are fortunately ignorant of the difficulties, underestimate them at the time of decision and start working with unimpaired optimism. However, not all difficulties are underestimated; paraphrasing Marx, Hirschman suggests that "mankind always takes up only such problems as it thinks it can solve".

Needless to say in less developed countries hiding difficulties has not always been beneficial. This is why many proponents of social cost-benefit analysis maintain that uncertainty should be reduced to a minimum in project design and carefully estimated. The point that Hirschman makes is that this may be counterproductive, since it may reduce the rate of investment, unduly increase the cost of planning, and harm the spirit of enterprise.

What happens in practice is a function of circumstances other than a conscious assessment of the "optimally unknown". There is still much too little capacity for estimating uncertainty. This is related not only to limited practical experience but also to insufficient knowledge of relevant theory. A study of project selection in Kenya, Zambia and Tanzania indicated "a surprisingly limited involvement of 'politicians' in micro-planning, including budget preparation" (20). An important reason is that "familiarity with the theory appears to be a decisive means to increase the validity and the reliability of the analyses and to determine what can be achieved and what cannot be achieved by applying the cost-benefit analysis" (21). The absence of such familiarity leads to "a 'filling-the-forms" application of the cost-benefit analysis with such a demand upon the analyst to cope with the mechanics thereof that the substantive part of the analysis might be oppressed" (22).

Essential improvements in the mechanics of project planning and execution require careful attention at all links in the chain of the project cycle. Yet project appraisal (the final estimate of profitability before an investment decision is taken) has been refined lately far beyond the means of practical applicability. Because of disagreements on the usefulness of "second best" methods, it has become a "fine art" rather than a practical craft.

## III. PROJECT SELECTION AND THE DICHOTOMY BETWEEN HARD AND SOFT SECTORS

As we mentioned earlier, problems of quantification and uncertainty bias investments and the use of scarce appraisal resources, which tend to go to hard sectors, such as hydroelectricity, transportation and other physical infrastructure (23). In "softer" areas, particularly those designed to help improve human capital or to obtain a more

equitable distribution of resources, benefits are much more difficult
to quantify. In such soft sectors as health, education, population
planning, nutrition and rural development which are concerned with
the organisation and development of human resources, assistance is
almost always necessary to develop domestic institutions.

In the soft sectors, the challenge in design is to identify projects
which are labour intensive, humanly satisfying and equity conducive,
and to try to make them profitable to the enterprise and/or the
nation rather than to identify projects which are commercially profitable and then make them labour intensive. All too often efforts to
introduce a "social component" into "productive" projects, intended
to make a profit, turns out to be counter-productive. In Tanzania,
for example, labour intensity on the Kilombero Sugar Estate proved
to be a threat to the viability of the Kilombero Sugar Mill. In its
report for 1975/76, the Tanzania Investment Bank pointed out that
"it is possible to reduce a number of workers in many factories
without affecting production. Screening of redundant staff can be
done both at factory or estate and holding corporation levels".
This suggests that even countries which, like Tanzania, emphasise
distribution are concerned that employment should be profitable. But
relations between employment and productivity are complex, and a
suitable compromise is difficult to find. A fertiliser plant may,
for example, increase local employment, but harm both income distribution and employment in surrounding areas if it encourages large-
scale farming methods which displace rural labour.

The dichotomy between hard and soft sectors is to a great extent the
product of the separation between technical and financial assistance.
Lenders have been concerned with collateral and repayment and have
therefore been inclined to favour "productive" rather than "social"
sectors.

Since capital went to hard infrastructure, there was more institution-
building and accumulation of power in the corresponding departments
and agencies than in those representing the soft sectors. There were
two reasons for this: first, loans had to be repaid, and there was
thus a risk for the lender that had to be minimised by careful planning and execution; institution-building therefore became part of the
loan arrangements. Second, the treasury was anxious to spend on sectors that could contribute recurrent income in the form of fees for
services offered, e.g. for water, electricity, transport and port
facilities, and to avoid recurrent costs for services like health
and education, which do not generate income.

Planning capacity and negotiating power thus developed in certain
sectors and not in others. In countries like Costa Rica, Panama,

the Philippines and Thailand, this power was so great that a substantial part of national planning came to reside in the departments of public works. The treasuries have usually been content when recurrent income has been secured and recurrent expenditures kept down. In this connection electricity has been more popular than irrigation and highways more popular than feeder roads, both with the lender and the treasury.

This has meant that while external agencies have been asking developing countries to take care of their social (or "basic") needs, the institutions and techniques to satisfactorily design and appraise such projects have not been found. External agencies have been reluctant to lend and developing countries reluctant to borrow.

IV. PROBLEMS IN THE DEVELOPMENT OF INDIGENOUS INSTITUTIONS

The consequence of this state of affairs (dependence and domestic power interests) is that in the majority of developing countries, there are now two systems of project planning, one domestic and one "alien". The demands made by foreign investors, lenders and donors are such that they absorb much of the local staff capacity for project design and analysis. The major share of investments, i.e. those financed by domestic resources, have therefore been handled by simpler criteria and evaluated by whatever capacity was left. This was justified by the opinion that knowledge would be transferred in the process. It appears, however, that an inadequate amount has been transferred, as the use of available domestic staff for duties shared with foreign experts and consultants has not brought about enough "learning by doing". The pressure for volume and the shortage of time did not allow for sufficient transfer. However, certain values have been ingrained, transferred into some institutions, and converted into budgeting practices.

The demands by external agencies for project evaluation and monitoring may well be counterproductive by their own standards because of the inadequacy of institutions and the scarcity of manpower.

External agencies must satisfy claims from their governments, auditors and public opinion and often have a scientific and managerial drive to acquire knowledge. Much domestic capacity is allocated to satisfying the demands of the most ambitious external agencies, sometimes in sensitive areas in the host country, which can cause resentment against dependence upon what is felt to be oversophisticated methods.

But it is not the degree of sophistication in itself that is the primary issue, but rather a disparity in competence resulting in studies that are often too difficult to understand, too demanding

to implement, and which therefore waste resources. In countries
where the administrative structure as a whole is not yet strong
enough, or where development problems are particularly serious or
urgent, a reaction against planning per se is generated by the disparity between what is proposed by external experts and what can
actually be done by domestic staff. The suspicion that commercial
motives are guiding the methods and volume of studies reinforces
this reaction.

To redress this situation, governments need to improve the quality
and quantity of their manpower. Training of local staff has not been
adequate even in sectors receiving substantial official and commercial credit. For foreign investors and commercial lenders there is
no related incentive, and development lenders have often been prevented by their statutes from engaging in technical assistance except on
a limited scale. The technical assistance offered has often been
biased  by the fact that consultants tend to prefer technical and
commercial solutions already tried in their own countries, which are
often difficult to adapt to a different cultural situation.

Project analysis is now taught in an increasing number of universities in the developing countries, largely as a result of initiatives
taken by bilateral and multilateral agencies (24). The Ford Foundation, the Inter-American Development Bank, the Organisation of
American States, the USAID and the World Bank (through its Economic
Development Institute) have been prominent promotors and suppliers
of training. In Europe the University of Bradford, supported by the
Overseas Development Administration of the UK, offers regular courses
in project analysis for students from developing countries; the
DSIE, the German Foundation for International Development, has also
been active in this field for many years.

No systematic assessment seems to have been made of the importance
of this training, except recently by the DSIE. The conclusion is that
it constitutes a significant contribution which would, however, be
greater if developing countries were more closely involved. Decision-
makers need to be convinced of the value of education in project
analysis, otherwise the incentive to study it will not be great
enough. In most developing countries the distance between decision-
makers and analysts is great because they have different constituencies and priorities.

Governments must give greater commitment to institution-building in
connection with staff training. Institutions are now dispersed and
coordination between them is poor. Very few countries, if any, have
made an effort to study the institutional and manpower aspects of
the problem of project planning and execution. Training must embrace
a great number of disciplines.

Formal education is only a first prerequisite for competence in project analysis. On-the-job training is vital and in the LDCs this is usually done under the guidance of external experts with the result that, as we have already outlined, the methods adopted are largely proposed, explicitly or implicitly, from abroad. The agents transferring methods of micro-planning are: the foreign private sector through investments involving industrial processing, licensing, equipment supply, marketing and management contracts; development leaders through financial support to domestic financial institutions (25), and consultants who serve all categories. Whether this is good or bad is a moot point; it is more relevant to enquire about alternatives. A further, internal, problem is that most developing countries find it difficult to attract and keep staff competent in project analysis because of the great salary differentials between the private and public sectors. Planning offices in many countries are under-staffed for this reason. Also trained project analysts tend to become operators at a higher level.

## V. CONCLUDING COMMENTS

In this chapter we have reviewed the issues which we believe to be the main determinants of the system within which decisions are taken on investment projects in developing countries, and have then discussed the nature and capacity of the institutions in this system.

The discussion has centered on project selection and financing as the critical area in which the issue of development is effectively decided; projects are the "cutting edge" of development (26). Design determines the degree of risk one is prepared to take, that is, whether one copies, innovates, preserves or consolidates. Design capacity in developing countries is improving but is still critically inadequate. Impartial advice on technology and the choice and use of consultants is therefore urgently needed. This is now offered on an ad hoc project by project basis which, to be effective, must be institutionalized. An ideal project institution is one that would make the conception of alternative projects and design possible. This requires a function similar to that of Research and Development in large enterprises. It exists within the World Bank, which is outstanding among bilateral and multilateral agencies in this respect; in developing countries it is rare. In the prevailing system, little attention is paid to alternatives except on an ad hoc intuitive basis. Once a project has been selected for consideration it generally ends up being implemented, usually with a conventional design.

A searching and systematic approach to project design requires changes in public administration. To meet social needs, planning should be interwoven with studies in pre-feasibility and project design in a multidisciplinary dialogue at several levels (27). Planning could then tend to become a single process encompassing the whole project cycle. It would be cumulative, incremental and iterative. This is of course an ideal, but it is an ideal that can suffer compromises and that can be approached organically from below. Essentially, the problem is one of evolving design, of formulating, considering and excluding alternatives as one proceeds towards a satisfactory solution. It will require a reconsideration of the roles of, and potential conflicts between, the players in the game (external agencies, consultants and domestic authorities at the central, regional, and local levels) on a larger scale and with more detailed coordination than hitherto. Conflicting interests that impede improved coordination must be overcome; the time factor and demands for documentation must not be counterproductive. The dichotomy between external and domestic methods and criteria must be resolved by anchoring the process within the developing country itself.

Some of these changes seem now to be in the making. Popular participation is recognized as urgent and may help resolve some bureaucratic constraints. It will take time but could lead to the application of simple and consistent criteria based on available data rather than the now often too sophisticated techniques based on unreliable or "invented" data. Political will is a requirement, but political will itself can be positively influenced by an appropriate system.

In summary, we have tried to show that in the absence of domestic capacity for project planning and implementation, alien criteria will unduly influence development. The ways in which decisions are made is determined by various vested interests, which affect the degree to which criteria for project appraisal are taken seriously.

CHAPTER III

PROJECT ANALYSIS IN DEVELOPING COUNTRIES: FIVE CASE STUDIES

We shall examine here the planning and appraisal methods in five
countries - Brazil, Nigeria, Peru, Tanzania and Thailand - and the
institutions they have built to carry out their projects. Though
their history, geography, resources and stages of development vary
widely, they all face the same problems as other developing countries: poverty, a rapidly expanding population, a precarious economic and political base and considerable dependence on external
forces.

In the Seventies, each was in the process of establishing a project
planning and analysis system, often a natural development of national planning, which illustrates the international trend we are concerned with here.

I. BRAZIL

In Brazil the President is formally in charge of national planning
and is advised by two councils of economic and social development.
The Planning Office (SEPLAN) was headed by a minister with a vice-
minister as deputy. It receives its inputs from the sectoral offices
of the functional ministries and corresponding offices at the local
level. Related public agencies and enterprises were found at both
levels. Other central features of the planning system were the
Institute of Statistics (IBGE), the Institute of National Planning
and Research (IPEA), the National Development Bank (BNDE) - which
played a major role as leader and coordinator of a national system
of more than 20 development banks - the National Research Council
(CNPQ) and the Pre-investment Fund (FINEP). The office of the Vice-
Minister for Planning was comprised, among others, of secretariats
for international relations (technical and capital assistance),
coordination with states and municipalities, administrative reform
and human resources, as well as technical offices for problems of
infrastructure, industry, and science and technology.

The national plan was established by law for a period of five years,
and was composed of sectoral and regional programmes, and such special plans as that for scientific and technological development.
The federal budget was approved by Congress for a period of three
years and revised annually. Apart from the federal budget, there was
a General Programme of Expenditures for enterprises and government
offices which were not financed by the Treasury.

In matters of development, Brazil has always been considered a special case because of its considerable size, volume of resources available for exploitation (land for agriculture and forestry as well as oil, iron ore, tin, bauxite, manganese), high growth rates in the past and considerable disparities in regional development and income distribution. The Second National Plan (1975-79) outlined a strategy for national integration designed to reduce regional disparities. In the following sections, we shall examine the project-planning process in Brazil in general terms and then describe the most important institutions in the process: the Industrial Development Council (CDI); the Pre-investment Fund (FINEP); the various regional development banks through which domestic development lending took place and which probably made the greatest contribution to project quality; and the special organisation involved with the development of the very poor Northeast region, SUDENE.

Ministries were responsible for project submission to SEPLAN (the planning office) for the annual plan and budget. They had their own guidelines but, except for certain departments, limited staff for preparation and analysis. In the opinion of Brazilian experts in training, the ministries and agencies involved in execution were, despite a large domestic training programme, too poorly staffed to meet desirable appraisal criteria.

Project work was primarily devoted to policy, coordination and some follow-up. No shadow prices, guidelines or appraisal criteria were prescribed, and project screening was confined to a few important projects for which careful cost-benefit analysis was done. Follow-up consisted of monitoring sector implementation with special attention again to the most important projects.

Federal planning agencies in the regions were responsible for coordinating state activities. In spite of considerable decentralisation on the state level, federal influence was strong, due to its financial power and policy instruments. Regional planning was large-ly a matter of establishing priority between and within regions. Generally conflicts of interest between regional and state authorities were resolved, accommodation being found in the name of 'compatibilisation". Decentralisation to the state level was expected to continue, and the federal planning agencies left a good deal of leeway to state agencies.

For example, the primary concern of the Sao Paulo planning agency was policy analysis and the choice of technology rather than project criteria, while industrial strategy was given more content. Incentives and support for appropriate and efficient production of goods and services had to be determined, and this required a proper

approach to the detailed problems of a number of subsectors. There
was some doubt about the value of specific foreign advice, but the
state planning agency had established contact with some advanced
institutes abroad. It was recognised that the transfer of relevant
technology would take place at the project level and that this would
require cost-benefit analysis and corresponding improvement in administrative procedures.

## A. Planning and Project Agencies in Brazil

### 1. The Industrial Development Council (C.D.I.)

The incentives for industry were established by the Industrial Development Council (C.D.I.) by reducing the cost of machinery and equipment for a project by more than 50 % through exemptions from various
taxes and duties provided for in Article 34/18. C.D.I. acted as a
project analysis agency, carrying out market, technical and financial
analyses, including the computation of internal financial returns.

Employment generation was also a criterion for granting incentives.
In the case of the North-East, however, the 50% income tax deduction
granted to encourage companies to invest so as to reduce unemploy-
ment was regarded by industries mainly as a "free risk", and investments were made primarily in capital intensive projects.

CDI had 25 professionals involved in project analysis, of whom 15
were economists and the rest engineers. The Council had problems
recruiting qualified staff because of higher salaries in the private
sector; for this reason, staff was seconded from state enterprises
to work with CDI. Project analysis was complicated by the fact that
Brazilian market conditions were heterogeneous and relatively unstable, which meant that data had to be revised at fairly short inter-
vals. Then, too, projects based on incentives quickly changed charac-
ter, and an important part of CDI's work was to monitor project implementation. Changes in international market conditions obliged CDI
to continually reassess the need for incentives and to see that they
were being correctly applied.

### 2. The Pre-Investment Fund (FINEP)

FINEP, begun in 1965 as a fund within the planning ministry, was
designed to finance studies and projects. In 1967 it became a public
enterprise and, in 1972, its mandate was expanded to include the
financing of government-approved studies and projects for all areas
of pre-investment, including science and technology.

The Fund was headed by a President and Vice-President, appointed by
the President of the Republic, who were members of the Advisory
Board, along with four other members appointed by the Minister of

Planning. The latter represented the BNDE, the IPEA, the CDI and the Central Bank.

Work was divided among five units: science and technology, non-conventional sources of energy, gas, project studies and research. The principal clients of the science and technology unit were universities and institutes, while the research unit concentrated on policy-making studies, and especially choices of technology.

By the mid-Seventies, about half of the total staff was professional and was comprised of engineers, economists, business administrators, geologists, lawyers and sociologists.


Loans were made almost exclusively to the public sector, and interest rates were low. However, FINEP also worked with a network of development banks in the regions and states, and these in turn lent primarily to the private sector.

The process of project identification at FINEP was informal. A client could request funds to finance a consultant study; consultants could request funds for equipment; or FINEP itself could initiate studies, even though its own staff for such work was small. The fund and the client then agreed on the terms of reference for a study. Screening of loan applications involved policy checks to see if the project fit national objectives; an administrative check on the client's previous work; a check on references and repayment terms; and a review of legal and contractual aspects. Monitoring and supervision included an examination of consultants' reports and projects implemented. No standard criteria had been established for project analysis, and project evaluation at market prices was considered adequate.

FINEP profited from technical assistance obtained in connection with financing by the Inter-American Development Bank. This was particularly important for the selection and utilisation of foreign consultants and the development of a corps of domestic consultants, an important aspect of FINEP policy.

Previous dependence on foreign consultants was said within FINEP to lead to "excessive capital imports, transfer of inappropriate technology, and insufficient domestic training and institution building". Expansion of FINEP's activities and the involvement of domestic consultants was supported by IDB loans for science and technology programmes. Loan terms usually included a component of technical assistance. An IDB requirement that at least three consultants be asked to bid on studies and projects made it difficult for FINEP to favour small consultants. Though the latter know local conditions

and relevant techniques, they did not have the resources to compete
with national or international firms. In order to promote a corps of
local consultants, FINEP therefore included in its programme direct
financial support to Brazilian consultant firms for as yet undevelop-
ed specialties. This support took the form of soft loans, used to
improve a firm's technical capacity and its ability to absorb new
knowledge.

3.    Development Banks

    a. The National Economic Development Bank (BNDE)
        BNDE lent primarily to the private sector, and application
instructions for BNDE loans were worked out in detail. For example,
the rate of investment had to be maintained, and volume was more
important than sophisticated analysis. The starting point was usually
a letter from a prospective borrower containing general information
about  its size, funds and loan requirements, and a request for consultation. Subsequent project evaluation covered financial, technical,
managerial and legal aspects and the effect on the balance of payments. Management, repayment capacity  and foreign exchange aspects
were particularly important. Shadow prices were not used, and no
rate for discounting was prescribed.

BNDE was well acquainted with theories of project analysis, and all
staff recruited had to have training in this area. However, in practice largely qualitative judgments were used. There was a guiding
notion that the discount rate ought to be of a given level, although
projects with a lower rate of return were sometimes approved. In
fact the rate of financial return was no absolute criterion, and was
not computed in all cases. It was considered more important to make
an overall evaluation as to whether the project was "valid for the
Brazilian development", i.e., whether it filled a need within the
whole complex of economic activities. An important consideration was
whether the project would create a nucleus of economic activity
generating more enterprises, particularly in an underdeveloped region.

In cases where there was clear evidence of price distortion, adjust-
ments were made to prices, but no parameters were established for
this purpose within the Bank. Distortions considered were primarily
in relation to the international market or through various fiscal
treatments. There was a notion of what the Brazilian exchange rate
ought to be, and adjustment was occasionally made on that basis.
Labour, however, was not shadow-priced and labour-intensive methods
of production were not encouraged per se. There was reluctance within
the BNDE to try to handle income distribution at the project level,
and it was believed that labour intensive methods often involved a
risk of losing the market. The emphasis was on obtaining the best

technology even though it might cause disequilibrium. Therefore, external development lenders often did not understand the special problems in Brazil, which sometimes made external criteria unsuitable in practice even though sound in principle. Nevertheless failure rates were low, and a contributing reason for this was the good quality staff who were paid approximately the same salaries as those in the private sector.

b. The Development Bank of Sao Paulo (BADESP)

Established in 1970, BADESP is the agent of FINEP in Sao Paulo and, in line with national and state objectives, its policy is to reduce regional disparities by selecting localities for new industrial plants beyond the already congested Sao Paulo area. Despite the very heavy emphasis on infrastructure and industries, BADESP claimed to make strong efforts to "identify and to correct sectoral distorsions".

Guidelines for project submission and evaluation were similar to those of BNDE, and appraisal included economic, financial, technical, managerial and legal aspects. No present value, break-even point, pay-back period and internal rate of return were computed with a discount rate and minimum rate of return. Shadow prices were used only occasionally, although tariffs and subsidies were considered in economic analysis.

Guidelines for feasibility studies had also been established, and the borrower was given a list of approved domestic consultants. BADESP themselves employed generalist consultants to help them analyse feasibility studies and assist Bank clients. A condition for lending was that borrowers accept assistance in accounting services, and courses were offered to clients. BADESP has experimented a general system of accounting for different agricultural subsectors with modifications for the special needs of individual sectors. Lines of credit offered were established after studies by private and official institutes. In agriculture, for example, continuous contact was maintained with the most important school of agriculture in the State of Sao Paulo and other institutes as well as the private sector. Farmers in the State of Sao Paulo had shown that they responded to selective incentives, and agriculture was therefore treated as a dynamic capitalist sector. However, in 1974, an examination of the economics of cotton production (a cash crop for export) uncovered a classic dilemma in project analysis: costs had exceeded revenue but the production function could not be changed in view of the already considerable investment in infrastructure and the absence of alternative production possibilities. It was clear that an uneconomic project was being funded. There was also a desire to meet general development objectives: directed investment was to be used to reduce migration to urban areas and to foster labour intensive projects. In practice this was proving to be very difficult.

### c. Banco do Nordeste (BND)

The poorest region in Brazil, the Northeast, has been given high development priority for more than a decade. The problem of poverty was attacked thanks to a high rate of economic growth, with special allocations for social sectors and special programmes of employment and income distribution.

BND had operational departments in agriculture, industry, and general short-term lending. In processing loan applications, a working group in the division of project analysis, consisting of an economist, an engineer and a lawyer, made a preliminary report and negotiations then proceeded with the borrower. Local consultants had taken over project preparation from BND, on the basis of its guidelines.

In computing rates of return, constant prices were assumed and inflation disregarded. Normally projects were analysed twice, in connection with preparation and just before lending decision, to recalculate profit and establish the loan amount. Since costs and receipts were uncertain, BND was more concerned with management and repayment capacity than with estimates of return and so the indicative discount rate was not mandatory. Shadow prices were not used for lack of data, and social cost benefit considerations were in terms of benefit recipients and required subsidies. In industry low interest rates were selectively applied and technical assistance given to promote growth in certain areas. In agriculture credit was given to small farms at subsidised interest rates.

BND conducted training courses in economic development in Fortaleza for some 500 decision-makers. In the beginning the centre concentrated on project analysis, but enlarged its programme to include the entire project cycle, including implementation.

There was considerable sophistication in project analysis at BND, but again circumstances led to a pragmatic application of techniques. Any project with feasible technology, market, finance, and administration was approved, and special programmes for housing, medicine, education, and nutrition were designed to improve equity. BND preferred to promote modern technology and competitive industries rather than labour intensity as such, and external agencies' concern with income distribution and employment was sometimes found irritating. Rapid growth was regarded as the best way to solve the employment problem.

d. The Superintendency for the Development of Northeast Brazil
(SUDENE)

SUDENE was established in 1959 for the purpose of stimulating investment in the Northeast. Initially it was funded by a 2%
federal tax revenue and contributions from the foreign exchange
premium, but operations were subsequently based on tax incentives.
There were two directorates for finance and personnel, and an executive secretariat assisted by an advisory board whose members included
the superintendent, the heads of directorates and departments, advisory staff and auditors. The project appraisal system was based on
an elaborate incentive system which included points earned by projects satisfying certain development criteria (1). Main considerations for approval of projects/incentives were location, employment
and use of local raw material and technology.

SUDENE participated in studies and the planning of large colonization
projects and monitored execution. Projects were prepared according
to guidelines established by the relevant federal agencies, e.g.
INCRA (The National Institute for Agrarian Reform and Colonization)
and GEIDA (The Group for the Execution of Irrigation and Agricultural
Development Projects). Sophisticated techniques of analysis had not
yet been introduced within SUDENE and no discount rate was established and rates of return were not computed. Project studies were
usually done by consultants, domestic and foreign. Screening was
largely in terms of relevant incentives; it is worth noting that
despite the social orientation of these incentives, income distribution in the Northeast since the establishment of SUDENE had gone
unchanged while per capita income doubled.

B. Development Objectives and the Domestic Capacity for Project
Appraisal

In spite of the fact that national planning as a formal exercise
emerged only with the development plan of 1972-74, project planning
and analysis in Brazil was comparatively advanced. Procedures and
methods had been worked out in detail and were used extensively,
particularly by FINEP and by the development banks. Training in
project analysis was extensive, and a domestic corps of consultants
of considerable size and competence existed.

The priority of economic growth and the high rate of investment put
greater emphasis on implementation than detailed analysis. Social
criteria were more prominent at the level of policy formulation and
resource allocation than in the analysis of individual projects.
Though foreign influence on investments and the transfer of technology was great, legislation had significantly increased domestic
control. In fact, the volume of technical and financial assistance
was relatively small and was on the decline.

## II. NIGERIA

Commanding a position in Africa similar to that of Brazil in Latin America, Nigeria has great potential for development. Though it derives much of its wealth from oil, an uneven distribution of natural resources and poverty in certain areas present serious problems, compounded by tribal and religious differences.

The first, second and third development plans covered the periods 1962-68, 1970-74 and 1975-80 respectively. The civil war of 1968-70 disrupted the progress of the first two plans. A progress report on the second plan showed considerable divergence between objectives and achievement (2), and one reason for this was thought to be the failure to obtain the expected foreign aid. Expected foreign aid for public sector investments in the first plan was 50% as against less than 20% received. For the second plan expectation was 20% and aid received was about 10%. The third plan was drafted therefore without expectations of foreign financial assistance. But there had been an over-reliance on oil revenues as a means of financing development, chiefly at the expense of agricultural development. In the Seventies, Nigeria had become a net food importer.

Planning at the Federal level was advanced, but the success of the planning effort depended largely on what was done at the regional and state levels. The presence of oil revenues led to a real planning-implementation gap and the third plan tried to work out a strategy that would reduce "the agonising delay in implementing major Federal Government industrial projects" (3). The capacity of the states for macro and project planning was considered inadequate. Most of the states had only one planner and depended heavily on foreign experts and consultants for project identification to be included in the plan. Often work did not proceed beyond the identification stage before funds were requested. State governments were not able to undertake feasibility studies on the majority of projects and for those few on which detailed preappraisal studies were carried out with a view to a private, usually foreign, partnership, such participation was difficult to secure. Therefore institutions were needed to translate plan objectives into projects and identify, appraise and monitor them.

## A. Project Planning at the Federal Level

The Economic Planning Unit of the Federal Ministry of Economic Development prepared a short manual on project preparation for the second development plan (4), requesting that "all project proposals and programmes will flow from the set of national objectives and priorities already spelt out (5). The Plan document itself referred to this manual and its importance in prescribing that "under no circumstance should a project be implemented without this pre-appraisal test" (6). The same view was expressed again in 1973 during the preparation for the third national development plan (7); for projects in industry, agriculture, transport and power expected to contribute to GNP, detailed appraisals were to be carried out to demonstrate their economic and technical feasibility (8).

Projects not directly productive were evaluated by using qualitative information, a summary of capital and recurring expenditure and their structure, revenue generated where applicable, and foreign exchange and employment implications.

Criteria for the identification, submission and selection of projects cannot be separated from national objectives and the state of development. Projects of reconstruction, rehabilitation and resettlement after the Civil War were added to those that would bring high rates of return, generate employment, substitute imports and bring sectoral and geographical balance.

A simple cost-benefit calculation of the project with a uniform discount rate was recommended. However, no detailed prescriptions were given for project appraisal, and the valuation of costs and benefits was not defined.

Identification of public projects at state and federal level was done by the executing ministries who forwarded their project proposals to the state and federal planning agency in the Ministry of Economic Development. State projects were then forwarded to the federal level where a joint planning board decided on their inclusion in the Plan. Public projects in the industrial sector were entered in the Plan on the basis of their economic viability calculated at market prices. Shadow prices were not used. Development banks sometimes assisted entrepreneurs in formulating acceptable proposals for potentially viable enterprises. Beyond the basic concept of viability, the criteria for project identification and selection contained in the official rules seemed to have limited practical impact. Procedures effectively followed and depth of analysis varied from one ministry or State to another. Implementation and follow-up often caused major difficulties.

B. Project Planning by Development Banks

National and State development banks and corporations played an important role in project appraisal. Some of them were not very explicit about procedures, the only criteria being that they finance economically viable projects in industry, agriculture, mining and commerce. However, the Kano State Ministry of Trade and Industry financed, according to its guide to investors, "development projects which are not likely to be financially profitable in the immediate future but which may be of economic benefit to the community". It further stated that it was "prepared to share in the cost of feasibility and market surveys and also to assist in the establishment of small pilot projects" and to help entrepreneurs formulate "acceptable proposals for potentially viable enterprises" (9).

The Nigerian Industrial Development Bank (NIDB) had to arbitrate between satisfying national objectives such as regional balance and income distribution and funding commercially viable projects.

As part of its indigenisation policy prescribing that loans below a certain level go to Nigerian rather than foreign investors, the Government exerted pressure to lend to domestic entrepreneurs. As projects tended to become smaller and less well prepared, bank overhead for evaluation increased. Moreover, it proved difficult to increase lending outside the Lagos area because there were less opportunities and higher risks.

## C. Consultants, Manpower Needs and the Role of Multilateral Agencies

Project-analysis procedures are strongly influenced by what consultants, development banks and aid agencies need or do. After 1974 efforts were made to use consultants and technical assistance as much as possible in project preparation. It was consequently not unusual to find consultants working with terms of reference which they themselves had elaborated. This made comparisons between projects analysed by different consultants very difficult, even though the quality of the work met professional standards.

Foreign development agencies contributed significantly to project analysis. The World Bank staff in Lagos was increased in response to the need for project identification and preparation. UNDP itself prepared most of the projects it sponsored, while the Ford Foundation has been involved in project preparation in Nigeria since 1960. The role of the official bilateral agencies was limited to appraisal of their own project activities, with the exception of USAID, which sponsored a training programme in project preparation and analysis.

Trained manpower was quite inadequate for a country of Nigeria's size and inflow of oil revenues. The nationwide training programme (around 180 trainees a year) was very small compared to the needs of the numerous federal and state ministries and public corporations. There was also a lack of technicians (engineers, architects, soil conservationists, etc.) to provide the technical inputs needed in project analysis.

Project analysis was still rudimentary in the Seventies not only because there was insufficient manpower but also because no uniform system of analysis existed. Dependence on foreign consultants was heavy and even the capacity to administer them was lacking, although the Nigerian Institute of Social and Economic Research had set up a Consultancy Service Unit to evaluate industrial projects and consultants' reports. Assistance from international development agencies was therefore badly needed both for handling consultants and for developing a project system with adequate staff resources. It was hoped that the emphasis on joint consultancy ventures would lead to the rapid rise of a corps of domestic consultants.

## III. PERU

Peru provides a marked contrast to the two countries examined so far. Following the military coup of 1968, Peru launched plans to bring about a socialist state: it wanted to reduce foreign influence; to create worker-managed industries; nationalize banks, the major export industries, petroleum refining and marketing, the fishing industry and the mass media; enact land reform and ensure a more even distribution of the means of production (10). However, in 1975, Peru was hit by an economic crisis, which contributed to a change in military rules and style of planning. Dependence on foreign capital markets became acute and, because of borrowing on a large scale, economic policy was influenced by external criteria. Partial denationalisation took place and new taxes were put on gasoline and exports.

A. National Planning and Project Analysis

In the Seventies, the infrastructure for planning and project analysis in Peru was one of the best in Latin America. In spite of considerable diversity among institutions dealing with pre-investment work - a characteristic of most developing countries- integration had come a long way towards a unified system. The dichotomy between macro-planning and projects was thereby reduced, and projects were developed in an increasingly logical and consistent way from national and sectoral plans.

The national planning system was comprised of the National Council of Economic and Social Development (CNDES) and the National Institute of Planning (INP) with sectoral and regional offices. The fact of having a sectoral planning office (OSP) within each functional ministry contributed to integrated planning and consistent methods of project preparation. INP established rules for pre-investment studies and project preparation in different sectors, and a major effort was made to set up procedures to train staff in project analysis.

The institutional system for the promotion of pre-investment studies necessary for project preparation and evaluation consisted of the Ministry of Economy and Finance for allocation of resources; INP and the sectoral planning offices for sector studies, plan elaboration and project identification; the special directorates of the functional ministries for project identification and supervision of studies; public enterprises for project identification and administration of studies; and state banks and development finance institutions, such as the development finance corporation (COFIDE) and the banks for industry, mining and housing for financing and supervision of studies. Pre-investment activities in the public sector were usually initiated by the special directorates, the sectoral planning offices and the state enterprises, which did the preliminary work on project proposals justifying their inclusion in national investment plans. The corresponding agencies for investments in the private sector were the state banks and development finance institutions.

Most project analysis was done at the sectoral level and even though the different sectors used separate sets of rules for project preparation, they followed a common pattern. The following summary of procedures used in industry is typical of the other sectors.

## B. Pre-investment Procedures in Industry

New investment possibilities were identified by OSP and the administrative departments in the ministry, the executing agencies (state enterprises) and COFIDE following the strategy and objectives laid down in the national plan (11). OSP gave priority to investment ideas so long as they were compatible with approved sectoral policies. Once an investment scheme was accepted in principle, OSP determined whether state participation was required. If it was not, the general directorate of industry established a project profile, listing all essential facts and figures, and tried to promote the investment in the private sector.

When state participation was requested, OSP either established a project profile or carried out a pre-feasibility study. The project could be dropped at this stage and for it to continue a ministerial resolution was necessary. As of 1972, the ministerial resolution commissioning the study to an executing agency in the industrial sector (e.g. INDUPERU) had to contain the terms of reference, profiles and previous studies, time schedule, budget and schedule of payments. During the study the executing agency had to report periodically to OSP, which checked whether the study was being carried out according to the terms of reference and the time schedule. The final report of the study had to be approved by OSP and the ministry (Alta Direccion) before the commission was officially terminated by a ministerial resolution.

Differences in project appraisal have been pointed out by Schneider:
"Note that the link between planning cycle and project appraisal
varies in strength according to the nature of the projects. Private
industrial projects will generally be defined independently from the
plan. But to get the investment permit they have to be presented to
and get the approval of the General Directorate of Industries (within
the Ministry of Industry and Tourism, MIT). However, the screening
of projects in this case is admittedly superficial and will rarely
result in a rejection or change of design as long as the project
lies within the broad lines of sectoral policies.

A somewhat more complete procedure is applied to public projects or
projects with public participation. Here the identification of a
project is often based on the initiative taken within the Ministry
which means that there is a direct link with sectoral policies and
objectives from the very beginning. Furthermore, these projects are
submitted not only to a sectoral appraisal but also to an appraisal
by the INP itself from the point of view of intersectoral priority.
This appraisal takes place before a project is presented to check
its compatibility with the budget"(12).

Despite basically adequate institutional arrangements, MIT pinpointed
a number of problems. These were:

1) insufficient operational capacity in the executing state enterprises;

2) absence of a system of evaluation which would allow more adequate
   decisions at the political level in all phases of a project;

3) lack of skilled manpower for preparation and evaluation;

4) weak position of the directorate general in relation to private
   industry;

5) duplication of work of financial institutions and with the sector;

6) insufficient coordination between the organisations involved in
   the pre-investment system;

7) lack of clear rules for the establishment of mixed enterprises;

8) disregard for the logical sequence of pre-investment, with the
   result that projects could not be rejected even if the analysis
   showed they were inadequate.

C. Methods of Project Analysis

The INP rules for project preparation (13) laid down in 1973 stressed
that the prime purpose of project analysis was to make sure that at
the project identification stage investments corresponded to sectoral and regional policy as defined in the national development plan.

Pre-feasibility and feasibility studies were also based on the relation between the project and sectoral objectives, targets and policies. The difference between a pre-feasibility and a feasibility study lay in the depth of information used; in a market survey, for example, the pre-feasibility study used only secondary information while primary data was collected for the feasibility study. Both included an economic justification, which could be called the appraisal in its strictest sense.

For both types of studies, the following were calculated: 1) profitability of the project as shown by present value of net benefits, benefit-cost ratio, internal rate of return, considering both total and domestic funds invested; 2) savings or generation of foreign exchange; and 3) capital intensity expressed as investment per man employed. For the feasibility study, a sensitivity analysis of costs and benefits of the principal variables was also carried out.

The rules did not stipulate how calculations should be made, nor was the problem of pricing mentioned (generally market prices were used). The role of taxes and duties was not explicated. Financial rather than social analyses were done. However, comparisons between appraisal results was difficult as no common rate for discounting costs and benefits was used. Usually more information than that listed above (from 1 to 3) and a sensitivity analysis was derived. For one major project, information on period of repayment, job creation, tax contribution and contribution to the social objectives and development strategy of the country were also computed.

Even when projects were appraised in such quantitative detail, the decision-maker still had to make his own value judgments. No attempt was made to relate the various predictions on project effects or to measure trade-offs.

D. The National Pre-Investment Fund and the Consulting Industry

In 1968 FINEPI (Fondo de Financiamento de Elaboracion de Proyectos de Inversion) was founded with IDB funding to build a coherent system of pre-investment studies and to develop a corps of Peruvian consultants. Given additional resources and expanded terms of reference in the Seventies, it was turned into COFIDE (Corporacion Financiera de Desarrollo), a development finance corporation designed not only to finance pre-investment studies but to foster the creation or modernisation of public and private enterprises. As such, it offered medium and long-term loans to all types of enterprises whose aims were congruent with those of the national plan.

In 1975 its pre-investment functions, previously handled by a sub-directorate of pre-investment and then by a sub-directorate for promotion were merged with the two divisions responsible for general operations and "propriedad social", companies to be run with increasing participation of workers. By then, the pre-investment fund had effectively been transformed into a development finance institution with a built-in lending function for pre-investment studies. This suggests that in Peru it was not possible or perhaps not desirable to develop an autonomous pre-investment fund with functions and responsibilities similar to those of FINEP in Brazil or FONADE in Colombia.

Though Peruvian pre-investment activities were scattered among various organisations and agencies using their own guidelines for studies and criteria for decision-making, great strides were made towards a national system: a law defining the project process of "propriedad social" was passed, and COFIDE set standards for studies and loans to the public and private sectors which were enforced.

COFIDE's own appraisal did not include technical aspects, which were checked by the prospective borrower and the relevant sectoral planning office (OSP), but confined itself to financial and economic aspects along INP lines.

It tried to give priority to domestic consultants, who usually had various working arrangements with foreign consultants. COFIDE drew up a consultants' register, but there was no legislation regulating the consulting industry. Nonetheless, the domestic corps of consultants grew and improved. By the end of November 1975, for example, 245 firms were registered, of which 73% were nationals.

## IV. TANZANIA

As in most developing countries, Tanzania's national objectives and its planning process determined to a large extent the nature of project appraisal and the institutional form in which it was carried out. Tanzania concentrated its development effort on the rural sector, its policy of socialism and self-reliance having been proclaimed in the famous 1967 Arusha declaration, which called for decentralised planning and participation, and rural mobilisation and transformation. Unlike many other countries, Tanzania has shown a willingness to take risks, to experiment and to develop new institutions in a situation where planning has become very complex.

## A. National Objectives, Planning and Projects

### 1. The Logistics of Decentralisation

Decentralisation of the government was a logical consequence of Tanzania's political ideology and its emphasis on rural development and the full utilisation of existing resources. The decision to decentralise, taken in July 1972, marked a significant change in the organisation of the national development effort and the system of planning and implementation. As the direct administrative powers of the Planning Ministry decreased, its role as coordinator grew: some of its functions were transferred outside the capital as separate agencies were established.

Decentralisation also led to changes in manpower and their location. A great number of senior and middle-level civil servants, including some 500 parastatal staff, were transferred from the capital to bolster regional and district administration. Civil servants working in the regions were made responsible to regional and district authorities; recruitment and allocation of staff, however, was still the responsibility of the Central Establishments Division in the President's Office. The chief political officer, the Regional Commissioner, was appointed by the President with Cabinet rank. The Regional Development Director's rank was equivalent to a Principal Secretary in the central Government and with similar responsibilities, including the function of accounting within the regions. Administration below the level of Director was divided into planning, finance and personnel. At the district level a similar organisation was headed by the District Development Director.

The Prime Minister's office (PMO) was also moved into the regions, becoming the centre of coordination and control, and professional staff were made responsible to their superiors in the regions and the PMO rather than the central ministry or agency.

Each district was divided into 30 to 40 wards and there was a continuous chain of development committees from the ward through the district and up to the regional levels. Laymen, civil servants and political functionaries were represented in development committees at all levels.

### 2. The Mechanics of Planning in the Decentralised System

Project identification and preparation became the main responsibility of the Directors at regional and district levels, who also supervised implementation once a project was approved. However, district and regional planning units were seriously understaffed and project planning tended to be ad hoc in nature. In practice a great deal of overbudgeting occured at the regional level and one of the main functions was budget screening. There was of course some central control on an annual basis; in principle priorities and targets were established and guidelines drawn up to facilitate planning; after suitable discussions an annual plan was drafted and submitted to the secretaries of the relevant ministries and regional development directors. During subsequent discussions the financial ceilings and allocations for each region and sector were established.

Establishing effective participation at all levels so that relevant capacity, experience and funds are available at regional and district levels  takes time.

The system contained elements of potential conflict between central and local authorities as taxation and appropriation remained the prerogatives and responsibility of the central Government. Responsibility for the implementation of projects with external bilateral or multilateral inputs also remained with the central Government.

B. The Nature of Project Analysis

Within the districts and regions, professional appraisal criteria were seldom applied; until 1976 cost-benefit estimates and rates of return were requested only for projects requiring loans from local banking institutions, in particular the Tanzanian Investment Bank (TIB) and the Tanzanian Rural Development Bank (TRDB). The National Development Corporation (NDC) was another important agency using project-appraisal criteria. We will examine the methods of all three institutions in the following sections.

Otherwise, choices were made on a project by project basis; sometimes, in order to secure the required funds, implementing agencies in districts and regions "committed" themselves by starting work on the site and ordering equipment.

1. Project Appraisal in Industry and the Role of the NDC

In the Seventies, industry played a relatively minor role in the Tanzanian economy. It was only in 1975 that Tanzania formulated an industrial strategy in line with its socialist objectives: a "choice of techniques should not be concerned with the factor-price frontier... but should be geared to satisfying socialist relations of production" (14). Necessary structural changes requiring some transfer of technology and skills had to be done in such a way as to avoid "reabsorption into capitalism" (15).

The National Development Corporation was the most important of the six parastatals (16) belonging to the Ministry of Commerce and Industry. It was designed to promote the development of, and hold interests in, the manufacturing and processing of leather and its products, alcohol and tobacco, paper, metals and a wide range of chemicals. National objectives dictated that NDC's investment programme emphasize projects using local materials and labour, and that the agricultural sector be expanded.

Standard project appraisal methods, including shadow pricing, were well known to NDC but identification, design and implementation were considered very complex and subject to many constraints. Project choice was determined on the basis of available opportunities. Ideas were usually generated within NDC, and projects took shape while looking for technical collaboration and partnerships.

The industrial Studies and Development Centre, set up in 1967 to deal with data problems and industrial studies, including project analysis, gave priority to on-the-job training and, given the large foreign-exchange expenditure on studies, recognized the importance of developing a corps of consultants. It was expanded in 1975 into a parastatal organisation called the Tanzanian Industrial Studies and Consulting Organisation.

## 2. The Role of the Tanzanian Investment Bank (TIB)

The Tanzanian Investment Bank and the Tanzanian Rural Development Bank, of which the government is the majority equity holder, were the guardians and promoters of project appraisal and indirectly of project preparation. Both institutions were heavily supported by bilateral and multilateral agencies, and their procedures and methods were influenced by those of the World Bank. Officials from the TIB and the TRDB attended courses at the World Bank's Economic Development Institute.

Since its founding in 1970, the volume of TIB lending has expanded rapidly, and a fund was established with development credits for consultancy services. Most of TIB loans were initiated by the clients themselves in a wide range of agencies and sectors.

Standard methods of project appraisal were used by a group that included an economist and an engineer or an agronomist. The financial, economic, management, technical and foreign exchange aspects of the project were examined. Shadow prices were used in only a few cases.

As its clients did not always have sufficient capacity, TIB became closely involved in identification, feasibility, design and implementation, that is, in almost the entire project cycle. The long period between identification and implementation, often prolonged by the requirements of external agencies, usually meant that conditions and costs had changed. Because some clients had poor capacity, TIB helped produce the documents which it later had to study and appraise. An important part of TIB's work was follow-up of each loan by monitoring and assistance to the borrower.

### 3. Project Appraisal in Rural Development and the Role of TRDB

Founded in 1971 as a successor to three agricultural credit agencies which had failed, the Tanzanian Rural Development Bank concentrated on loans to cooperatives and encountered less problems in recovering overdue loans than its predecessors.

The position, procedures and methods of the TRDB resembled those of TIB but its field of operation - underdeveloped rural areas - was more complex. After review at the local level, appraisals were carried out at headquarters with a more concise version of World Bank criteria. Usually the internal financial return was computed against a cut-off rate. The net present value or cost-benefit ratio was seldom computed. Economic analysis was done only for large projects. Shadow prices were seldom used, and a shadow wage rate was never applied; when external agencies introduced shadow prices, this was accepted as a concession.

TRDB produced a manual of policies and procedures (17) in which a project is defined as economically viable if it "generates more value than it uses over its estimated lifetime" (18). It is clear from this manual that the government gave TRDB considerable power to implement the rural development programme. Since this task was beyond its capacities in the Seventies, external agencies sometimes played an important role in project preparation.

Both TIB and TRDB encountered a problem common to all development banks: how to promote projects designed to alleviate poverty and improve income distribution when such projects are often not "bankable". For example, though TIB was involved in projects all over the country, the majority tended to concentrate around the major cities; it will take time for the communally operated Ujamaa villages to respond to investment opportunities.

Tanzania's emphasis on self-reliance should be seen in relation to its dependence on external resources and assistance which, in the case of project analysis, was still great. Consistent efforts were made to improve domestic capacity in all categories, including local consultants. But in purchasing and managing foreign advice and services, Tanzania was guided by clear political and economic development objectives.

## V. THAILAND

In Thailand, the private sector was strong although, by tradition, planning and decision-making have been concentrated in the central government. Project analysis was carried out by a number of different agencies, public and private, whose activities varied accordingly.

### A. The Role of the Central Planning Agency, NESDB

The main responsibility for national planning rested with the central planning agency, NESDB, in the office of the Prime Minister, which had power to manage and intervene in the entire project cycle, including domestic and foreign inputs. To remedy insufficient institutional arrangements for systematic planning, NESDB issued a set of guidelines in October 1974 for project preparation, appraisal and decision-making covering the technical, engineering, financial, administrative and environmental feasibility of a project as well as its relevance to national objectives.

Project appraisal within NESDB was based on work done by the individual ministry departments; about half of the staff were professionals. Consultants were used to appraise large, complex foreign-financed projects while domestic projects were appraised with simple methods. There was no consistent use of shadow prices, and data for their computation were not available.

NESDB work on project analysis for state enterprises was done in connection with submissions by the ministries to which the enterprises belonged. Coordination of these enterprises was difficult because several in the same sector reported to different ministries. The policy of each enterprise was formulated by its own Board of Directors, appointed by the Cabinet.

### B. Project Appraisal in the Ministries

Contacts between the ministries and NESDB were largely confined to pre-feasibility and feasibility studies. In the area of transport, which was an important sector in Thailand (19), the Department of Highways had built up considerable capacity in collaboration with a foreign consulting firm. The original consultancy was for road construction, but the services developed into institution-building, including organisation and management. Methods of preparation and appraisal, based for the most part on the World Bank model, were taught to the local staff. They included a shadow price for labour and considerable attention to labour-intensive methods of construction.

In the Ministry of Agriculture substantive work on project analysis started in early 1974, impetus once again having come from the World Bank; the head of the Planning Division and his assistant had both attended courses at the Bank's EDI. Analysis work was seriously hampered by lack of staff and data. Proposals from departments in the ministry were submitted to the Under-Secretary through the Planning Division, which was responsible for appraisal.

## C. Project Appraisal in the Private Sector

### 1. The Board of Investment (BOI)

Roughly two-thirds of all investments made in Thailand were in the private sector. The Board of Investments screened most of the large projects involving new investments with a view to granting incentives in the form of tax concessions.

The main concerns of BOI were employment creation and foreign exchange generation. Social rates of return were not computed; this was not only a question of time but because the BOI believed it could not make the relevant assumptions. The applicant himself had to show an internal financial return, and this was checked by BOI project analysts. BOI's primary task was to assess whether a market existed and how many firms should enter it. The problem of suitable technology was left to the investor. Income distribution concerns were incorporated by way of special privileges for selected industrial branches and geographical areas. No weighting procedures were used.

### 2. The Industrial Finance Corporation of Thailand (IFCT)

The IFCT was established in 1959 with loans from the World Bank, Japan, Germany and the USA. It was authorised to finance all projects approved by the BOI. Project appraisal in IFCT was by and large confined to financial analysis based on five-year projections of relevant payment streams. Neither discounted cash flow nor social cost-benefit analysis was done.

As a development bank, it was responsive to government objectives even though it was a private corporation serving the private sector. Government participation was maximised at one third, and the principal shareholders were commercial banks.


Formal procedures and methods of project planning and implementation in Thailand were sound but complicated by a large bureaucracy. In practice the project system was hampered by a lack of qualified manpower and by serious problems of administration and coordination.

The central planning agency did not as yet have the necessary staff resources and authority to make it completely effective, something that would also require improved capacity in most of the planning units in the ministries and departments. Given the strong position of the ministries, public projects tended to be identified and prepared according to different lines.

Given the predominance of the private sector, there was a need for government policy and incentives to identify projects that would coincide with such national objectives as employment and income distribution. Decentralisation was posing a serious challenge to an already strained public administration.

## VI. GENERAL CONCLUSIONS ON CASE STUDIES

Project planning and analysis in these five countries can be seen as a logical extension of national planning, a plan being only as good as its projects. Although little use was made of project analysis in most countries, proper analysis could potentially bring great benefits, as prices of productive factors were distorted. As a rule, exchange rates were overvalued, which discouraged exports; interest rates were low, leading to capital intensive methods of production; and food prices were low, favouring the urban population at the expense of farmers. Unskilled labour was abundant and, in relation to the opportunity cost, overpaid. On the whole pressure on the marketplace was overwhelming, and production was designed to meet demand.

However, momentum had been created and it was bringing steady improvement in development capacity, largely through development assistance. Improvements were made: departments and agencies had some trained staff and some necessary institutions had been created or reorganised under the influence of leading development lenders, notably the World Bank and the regional development banks, which replicated their own functions within state banks and enterprises.

Growth of domestic capacity was slow, since staff and institutional requirements could be met only gradually. In analysis speed often took precedence over care. There were several reasons for this: staff was not always available, as trained personnel often went to other positions; new design and analysis, notably for rural development, were difficult; functional departments resisted planning in much the same way as central planning agencies resisted external demands; and, last, the advantage of improved analysis was not always clearly perceived as the selection of projects was not directly related to the process of project analysis.

Institutional arrangements, including effective management of consultants, are necessary if there is to be innovation. The countries
described here have all encountered the same basic problem, which
they have dealt with in various ways. Banks and consultants have
everywhere played a prominent role; in Brazil and Peru, pre-
investment arrangements have gone furthest.

It was not until financial institutions in the developed countries
were ready to give priority to poverty and social justice as such
that a corresponding emphasis was fully accepted in similar institutions in developing countries. Even then, economic realities and
financial policies set definite limits as to what could be done to
promote development by lending proper.

CHAPTER IV

THE ROLE AND INTERESTS OF SOME EXTERNAL PARTIES

For domestic authorities and aid agencies alike, the problem of
development is to a large extent one of allocating resources wisely
and generating sound investment projects. This implies continuous
arbitration between speed, volume and quality. For the developing
countries attracting resources and getting the job done has tended
to take precedence over careful planning of individual projects,
while the policy objectives of aid agencies have implied, directly
or indirectly, a search for projects to support, where volume targets conflict with quality requirements.

Complaints have been raised by developing countries about intervention, subjective criteria and prestige projects resulting from external influence. On the other hand, efforts by external agencies
to introduce stringent criteria for project selection have not always
been appreciated, since they tend to delay investments. The use of
foreign consultants for project design has also come in for criticism; authorities in developing countries have claimed that they
transfer the wrong technology, while domestic consultants protest
that they pick the most attractive work out of the consultancy market. External auditors play a significant role but have received
less attention.

The present trend towards integrated programming, strongly influenced by aid agencies and combined macro- and micro-elements, implies
institution-building for the establishment of a national project
system guided by consistent criteria. We shall examine bilateral
agencies in general and then analyse the work of three multilateral
agencies: the Inter-American Development Bank, the United Nations
Development Programme and the World Bank.

I. THE ROLE OF BILATERAL AGENCIES

The role of bilateral agencies in project appraisal can be seen as
three sets of interrelated problems: the circumstances at home and
abroad  that surround the roles of aid; projects as a form of aid;
and the criteria used in the selection of these projects.

A. Foreign Aid and Projects: Donors and Recipients

Aid is given for a number of reasons - political, commercial, cultural and humanitarian. In practice the interests of donors and
recipients are rarely identical. Donors cannot seem to abstain from

looking at how resources will be used and their development effect.
Nations often continue to act in their own self-interest and aid
remains an aspect of foreign policy and foreign trade. To some extent all donors are guided by considerations of what kind of civi-
lisation to promote. Former colonial powers can use aid to exert
influence on their ex-colonies and big nations try to maintain the
balance of power (1).

Donors tend to apply conventional project criteria that stress
technical aspects and financial viability. Statements in national
assemblies to the effect that aid is a paying proposition are not
uncommon, and they illustrate the fact that progressive project
criteria are hard to apply in practice, even though they may be
accepted in principle both by aid administrators and host government
officials. Aid-tying is still prevalent and it often influences project selection and design.

Some donors concerned with filling basic needs and generating equitable development effects, either within the existing Western capitalist framework or within stated socialist objectives, have chosen
to work with countries whose policies give priority to such objectives. But a number of problems arise for such donors: the technical
and political aspects of such a strategy, poor capacity for project
design in these sectors, and a donor constituency that wants the
end product of aid to be clearly identified.

Since aid serves two masters it creates ambiguity, confusion and
ambivalence. A common format for project submission has long been
regarded as potentially useful but still remains to be worked out
and negotiated.

There is a strong professional case for the project approach, particularly as long as domestic capacity is inadequate. For the majority
of developing countries the preparation of projects in industry and
rural development presents both technical and human problems.

B. Bilateral Aid and Project Criteria

Criteria for and  the practice of project analysis are likely to
differ among bilateral agencies and also to differ within agencies
and over time. The priority of project analysis depends, on the one
hand, on internal professional criteria and audit requirements and,
on the other hand, on the degree of emphasis on the transfer of
knowledge and the effects on development. Risk avoidance is a concern for all parties involved, and in the program of each bilateral
agency, the order of aid priorities has to be understood in order to
see clearly the function of project analysis in context.

The political advantage of pressing stringent project criteria upon the recipient is negligible  but the political cost is not. A direct commercial advantage exists only where the donor has a stake in the project or where the project  brings orders for services and equipment. But any aid project may indirectly have a positive or negative effect on commercial relations. A difficult agency may jeopardize export orders as relations deteriorate. On the recipient side, there are thus few incentives for project analysis beyond a strict financial analysis.

But it is noteworthy that for bilateral agencies, incentives for stringent project criteria based on progressive policy are rare: it is more important to avoid criticism (from the government, auditors, press and the public) than to invite approval, as even the latter may give rise to criticism.

Developing countries tend to accept external criteria as a condition for obtaining aid, avoiding direct involvement in the actual design and analysis beyond a reasonable minimum agreed upon with the aid agency and the consultants and experts engaged in the project.

Project-analysis methods proposed by donors have found easy acceptance neither in their own agencies nor in the developing countries. Some bilateral agencies find it difficult to apply their own criteria to the preparation of "their own projects", and they have therefore not actively worked for their adoption in the developing countries. The Overseas Development Administration of the United Kingdom, for example, have recommended their Guide to consultants and developing countries, but its preface contains a warning that "any attempt to apply the Guide in its entirety is almost certainly foredoomed to failure" (2). Other agencies have informed developing countries of their own criteria without recommending them. In general, external criteria will be enforced in the developing countries to the extent that they are mandatory at home. As a rule a pragmatic approach is taken, with due consideration to constraints both at home and abroad.

Bilateral agencies concerned with overall development effect usually make some estimate of national profitability. In theory no one disputes the value of social cost-benefit analysis, but in practice it has led to unresolved arguments about methods, which raise fundamental issues of development philosophy and the aid relationship. Since rigorous quantitative analysis is impossible, the argument has come to center on whether simplified methods are justified and if so, which ones. The simplest and most common method is to make common-sense estimates based on certain criteria with quantification limited to available data.

A practical distinction has been made between "economic" and "social" projects (3) : financial returns are computed where this is possible while the least cost method is used for projects not intended to be managed as income-generating enterprises. A substantial number of bilateral projects are for social infrastructure and do not easily lend themselves to economic analysis.

In the Seventies bilateral agencies paid increasing attention to income distribution and to environmental aspects. Quantitative analysis of these two aspects generally dealt with expected effects of the project on employment, on the income of relevant social groups, and on the surrounding environment and the wider ecology.

The search for simplified methods and procedures continued, and the trend among bilateral agencies was towards a more global approach, leaving greater responsibility for project planning and execution to the host country. This was motivated both by increasing domestic capacity in the developing countries and pressure on aid agencies for improved delivery. Two serious constraints will remain, however, until relations between development partners have been normalized: donor audit requirements and host country capacity for planning and execution. It has been said repeatedly that institutional change in the developing countries is a prerequisite for desired development. It is less often said that a similar change in donor institutions may be a prerequisite for improvement in the aid relationship.

## II. The Role of Multilateral Agencies

We shall now turn to three multilateral funding agencies: the Inter-American Development Bank (IDB), the United Nations Development Programme (UNDP) and the International Bank for Reconstruction and Development (IBRD), popularly known as the World Bank. The charters of both the IDB and the IBRD prescribe that lending should be for projects, and the UNDP, formed as it was from the consolidation of the Special Fund and the Expanded Programme of Technical Assistance, is involved in project funding and related pre-investment activities, usually in association with other UN agencies. In particular we shall examine how the funding activities of these organisations have led, directly or indirectly, to the development of project-appraisal institutions in developing countries.

## A. The Inter-American Development Bank (IDB)

When the IDB was formed in 1960, borrowing member countries were from the start contributors to the Bank and shared responsibility for policy and decisions on priorities, lending and technical cooperation. Technical assistance was also provided for in the Agreement establishing the IDB.

## 1. Pre-investment Lending by IDB

The countries that have received global pre-investment lending (which the borrower can use for relending or for financing individual studies) vary widely in size and level of economic and social development. The main recipients of pre-investment lending have been Argentina, Brazil, Colombia and Mexico.

Lending to pre-investment funds and agencies was prepared for, and supported by, a good deal of technical assistance for institution building, especially to ministries of planning. A minimum of institutional infrastructure and absorptive capacity is necessary if pre-investment funds are to be meaningful. IDB experience shows that the more developed a country is, the greater the contribution of a central pre-investment agency becomes. On the other hand, central investment agencies can themselves promote development and institution-building. The basic argument for the establishment of national pre-investment agencies can be summarised as follows. Project generation is still a primary concern both for the lender and the borrower. The volume of lending that a borrower can attract is directly related to the volume and quality of projects prepared. Project preparation in turn is functionally related to the volume of financing available at the time a project is ready. It is important for the borrower to establish a mechanism to shorten the period of financial negotiation with external agencies. A "pipeline" of projects facilitates financing, makes choice of alternatives possible and improves the composition of the investment programme as a whole.

IDB has been involved substantially in diagnosis and programming at national and sector levels, and the best way to "decentralise" its own work on projects was to help establish central pre-investment institutions. The original objective was that each country's central planning agency play an important role in the management of the pre-investment institution and that intermediary financial development institutes look after the private sector. However, in practice the weakness of the newly established planning agencies led to difficulties in allocating available pre-investment funds as intended. In some cases the relending process took place about 30 months beyond the agreed period of loan commitments; in other cases IDB had to cancel uncommitted balances. There were also differences in capacity between agencies working in different areas of the public sector.

IDB tried to promote pre-investment funds and agencies with sufficient autonomy to impose criteria for balanced allocations, integrated planning and coordinated implementation. For example, Colombia's FONADE and Brazil's FINEP are entirely autonomous.

In other countries funds were set up within ministries of planning or development banking institutions. FONEP in Mexico has a trustee relationship with Nacional Financiera S.A., which in turn has broad autonomy. In Chile the national pre-investment fund was established within CORFO, the National Development Corporation. In most cases, IDB and its borrowers agreed on a considerable amount of technical cooperation to strengthen both ministries of planning and related pre-investment funds and agencies.

As a rule loan conditions were tied to the parallel creation of a central pre-investment institution, and in the agreement between IDB and the borrower, a great number of details were codified as prerequisites for success. At first, a great many problems cropped up, delaying IDB disbursements and host country loan commitments. This was not surprising in view of the great difficulty in setting up a central institution for which no previous experience existed.

A number of technical aspects had to be defined, prepared for and mutually understood, For example, the institutional machinery in some borrowing countries was too complex, control systems were inadequate, responsibilities were fragmented, and the selection and contracting of consultants was hampered by lack of experience. Some studies were abandoned because of deficient methodology, while controls and requests for information from IDB were sometimes felt to be excessive. Often domestic administrative deficiencies were not identified and attended to early enough; in particular, many domestic executives did not fully understand the objectives and procedures of the pre-investment activities designed by IDB and the borrower. Once these difficulties were ironed out, the rate of IDB disbursements increased rapidly.

## 2. Developing Domestic Consulting Capacity

The need for consultants goes hand-in-hand with that of national pre-investment funds or agencies. In many countries financing is rarely available at short notice, so private and public entrepreneurs have had to depend on short-term bank credit to finance project preparation and execution, which ideally should be made on a medium- or long-term basis. This in turn led them to depend on credit from foreign suppliers who could offer a package deal, including project preparation and evaluation, financial credit as well as goods and services.

The disadvantages are obvious: it is difficult to know whether the price and quality of equipment are competitive and what the actual cost of financing is. And as no independent feasibility study is done, there is no guarantee that the solution is the most appropriate.

both technically and economically. Such a situation tends to foster the indiscriminate acquisition of imported technologies and capital goods and the inefficient use of human and natural resources. Unfortunately a good many investment projects are too small to justify international competitive bidding.

This vicious circle can be broken only by increasing domestic capacity and expanding domestic markets. In Latin America, for example, the growth of consultant firms, stimulated in part by the IDB pre-investment global lending programme, has been spectacular: in 1966 about 300 consultant firms were registered with IDB; a decade later, the figure had jumped to some 1,500. A substantial amount of regional technical cooperation now takes place, and such large, experienced funds as FONADE (Colombia), FINEP (Brazil) and FONEP (Mexico) can offer technical assistance to other Latin-American pre-investment funds.

Borrowing countries have greatly benefitted from having specialized agencies coordinate their pre-investment work and their relations with international financing agencies and other sources of external credit. Central pre-investment funds and agencies were designed primarily to finance studies of smaller, less technically complex projects for which local consultants were qualified. As this increased the speed at which investments could be generated, it started a process by which domestic capacity grew constantly. To further this development, IDB served as adviser to agencies as well as public and private enterprises.

An important aspect of IDB assistance has been to help prepare lists of domestic consultants and to offer guidance in dealing with foreign consultants. When IDB first used a Latin-American consulting firm for inspection and supervision in another Latin-American country, the initiative met with surprise and resistance. Today, when a foreign consultant gets a contract, he usually spends half on local sub-contracting, and more and more often the "foreign" consultant is a Latin American. Many firms have become so competent that they have won contracts outside the continent, working in such countries as the Philippines, Morocco, Algeria, Sudan, Turkey and West Africa.

### 3. Sectoral Allocations and Domestic Project-Appraisal Capacity

The social orientation of IDB lending was consecrated in the Charter through the establishment in 1960 of a Fund for Special Operations, which was the "soft window" corresponding to the International Development Association (IDA) of the World Bank. Since IDB was founded, "soft" lending has amounted to more than half the total. Loans are made on concessional terms for land settlement and improved land use, housing for low-income groups, community water supplies and sanitation facilities, and supplementary financing of advanced-education facilities.

IDB's concern with social progress called attention not only to certain social sectors in individual countries but also to the poorest of its member borrowers. Here the need for domestic capacity for project preparation and appraisal proved doubly urgent for, just as economic sectors with the capacity for project planning tend to attract funds, the member borrowing countries which are most advanced in national and project planning tend to attract a disproportionate share of available funds. IDB's efforts to help build domestic institutions suitable for project generation were prompted by the Social Progress Trust Fund, which made loans available for sectors where planning capacity had not yet developed. It gradually focussed its efforts on central pre-investment institutions in the borrowing countries, all the more so because this was found to be an effective way to develop a corps of local consultants. Countries without domestic capacity for project preparation have to rely on foreign consultants, which is not only expensive in terms of foreign exchange but may also introduce a potential bias in priorities and technology.

In the public sector, a weak planning agency also affects the allocation of available pre-investment funds. In the absence of strong leadership and coordination, the departments and agencies dealing with infrastructure (power, energy, transport) not only balk at using the criteria of the central planning agency but also attract most of the funds. Consequently studies and related developments in the "soft" sector are delayed.

4. Two Case Studies of Pre-investment Funding

In the comprehensive review of project planning (Chapter Three), we looked briefly at the role of two Latin-American pre-investment funds, FINEP in Brazil and COFIDE in Peru. Here we shall confine ourselves to pre-investment funding as it was seen in FONADE (Colombia), the third largest pre-investment fund in Latin America and CBF (Bolivian Development Corporation), one of the smallest funds in one of the poorest countries.

a) The Colombian fund FONADE

The history of FONADE is an interesting study in autonomy. In 1963 the U.S. Government through AID made a soft loan to Colombia for project generation via the planning commission in Bogota. Four years later, the $3 million was barely touched, and a Colombian civil servant recently returned from IDB in Washington was asked to make suggestions as to how this money could be used to speed up the investment process. A unit was established in the President's Office for the purpose, and a special projects group was formed on the basis of a contract between the Central Bank and the President's Office. The group had limited experience in project appraisal, and AID terms of reference were constraining; among other things, a list of 10 consultants for each study had to be drawn up and then approved by AID, and AID reserved the right to review consultancy contracts for individual studies. It was also stipulated that all studies were to be carried out by American firms.

After negotiations with the U.S. authorities, Colombia was given greater authority to administer the funds, and two model contracts were worked out to fit most situations. After some time all the funds were committed for studies.

The agreement with AID was modified so that half the funds were to go to American consultancy firms and the other half to Colombian firms. In practice, consortia were set up between U.S. and Colombian firms, which gave impetus to the development of a consultancy industry in Colombia.

When AID funds were exhausted, the special projects group realized it had neglected to arrange for further financing through some form of rotating funds. Colombia then asked IDB for funds and in 1968 established FONADE. At first the agency needed approval from the Ministry of Planning and the Central Bank each time it wanted to disburse funds for pre-investment studies. However once FONADE had developed its manpower and established contacts in ministries, it became autonomous and in practice acted as a public investment corporation rather than a fund.

The support of the President during this process of institution-building was essential. All ministries and agencies were requested to forward copies of previous pre-feasibility and feasibility studies to FONADE, which thus became a data bank for pre-investment studies.

IDB and the World Bank provided guidance on management of the fund: for example, how to collect information, draft terms of reference for consultants, supervise studies, improve accounting systems and price services. Close relations with the Treasury and the Planning Ministry resulted in improved allocation of resources.

However, borrowers disliked the rather strict contracts formulated by FONADE and the fact that they had to pay interest on money needed for studies, so a good number turned to other sources, including the Treasury, for funds. It was therefore decided that all pre-investment studies had to be done on a loan basis through FONADE;

if the individual agency had funds of its own, FONADE was authorised
to supervise the studies, including terms of reference for hiring
consultants. For external finance, however, the Treasury alone was
authorised to negotiate, with technical support from FONADE.

FONADE quickly became one of the most prominent pre-investment institutions in Latin America, giving technical assistance and advice to
other Latin-American governments. Its own staff of full-time professionals was supplemented by staff from the National Planning Agency.

Normal FONADE procedure for selecting and contracting studies ran
as follows: a technical committee with representatives of the Planning Agency and FONADE decided whether the study could be financed
or not; if the decision was positive, terms of references were drafted and a committee on projects with representatives from both bodies
maintained contact with the relevant agency (which was not represented on the committee); FONADE supplied the agency with a list of approved consultants, whereupon the agency invited proposals for the
study; the proposals submitted were judged on the basis of guidelines
established with FONADE, and the consultant was chosen; FONADE followed the study through progress reports,and disbursements were related
to these reports; the final study was approved by the Planning
Agency, FONADE and the relevant public agency or private enterprise.

When external financing for the project was identified in advance,
it also participated at some point in the study.

## b) CBF, the Bolivian Development Corporation

Bolivia received its first pre-investment global loan from
the Inter-American Development Bank in 1966 but a number of problems
prevented CBF from developing rapidly into a national pre-investment
agency. The Executive Pre-investment Committee could not be constituted, and this affected working relations with IDB, which was to
have a representative on the committee. The disbursement schedule
agreed upon could not be met and had to be extended by two and a
half years. One-fifth of the studies were to be for the private sector but the figure was not met. The drafting of terms of reference
for consultants presented difficulties and this held up competitive
bidding; in practice only a single consultant firm could be used,
which in turn made consultants less interested in submitting bids.

National pre-investment studies were confined largely to industry
and mining, although this was due to national budget allocations
rather than to a shift in CBF priorities. Nonetheless the planned
number of studies was in fact carried out even though disbursements
were delayed and some changes in the programme made.

To help Bolivia solve its pre-investment problems, IDB then entered into technical cooperation on a grant basis for the establishment and implementation of a National System of Planning and Projects, consisting of the following governmental bodies: the National Council of Economic Planning (CONEPLAN), the chief decision-making body in the National System; the Ministry of Planning and Coordination of the Presidency, the normative, coordinating and supervising body acting in pre-investment through a National Institute of Pre-Investment (INALPRE); the Ministry of Finance, which received, allocated and controled the National System's operating funds through a National Institute of Finance (INDEF); and the sectoral organisations responsible for project formulation and execution.

INALPRE, established in 1974, became the main body for coordinating and guiding pre-investment activity and for financing project studies and therefore the principal project-appraisal institution.

To strengthen the newly established institutions, a detailed programme of technical cooperation was agreed upon with IDB, with provisions for experts and short-term consultants in all related professional fields (financial, economic, technical, administrative and sociological).

## B. The United Nations Development Programme

The United Nations Development Programme (UNDP) was set up in late 1965 as a consolidation of the Special Fund, whose job had been to accelerate economic development in the less developed countries, and the Expanded Programme of Technical Assistance. The basic purpose of the UNDP was to integrate and coordinate the development assistance activities of the UN and the Specialized Agencies and to meet the objectives of developing countries more efficiently and effectively.

When a Government requests assistance from the UNDP, it may announce its intention to execute the project itself. The Government in question must then inform the UNDP office of the Executing Agency (usually a UN Specialized Agency with investment units, such as FAO, UNESCO, WHO or UNIDO), but in each case the decision will be taken by headquarters. It also provides the UNDP with "information on the technical and managerial capability" of its own executing agency: in particular, the domestic institution's experience in executing similar projects financed either by domestic or external resources; its technical experience and know-how and its access to, and links with, national and international sources of expertise; its ability to exercise adequate managerial and administrative supervision of the project and its internal budgetary, accounting and audit arrangements.

The Government request, which will be forwarded by the Resident Representative to the Regional Bureau with relevant comments, will provide information on development and project objectives, background and justification, total cost and proposed UNDP contribution, planned outputs and required inputs. The Regional Bureau will review and appraise the request, and it may then recommend additional measures by the executing agency in order to "strengthen its capability and promote self-reliance". If the Government request is not accepted, the Regional Bureau will "make alternative recommendations to the Government for implementation of the project".

An important point is that the UNDP decision to assist a given project is distinct from the decision to grant Government execution. Project design and appraisal will thus not be held up by the decision on project execution. And the UNDP may on request supply services required for project formulation. With the agreement of the Government, UNDP may supplement its own resources with those of "the appropriate Specialized Agency or other organisations in the United Nations system, or private consultants, consultancy firms or other organisations, including universities, development institutions or voluntary non-governmental organisations". Another important point is that "the process of appraisal will be undertaken in accordance with the arrangements laid down in the Manual".

All this suggests that UNDP will retain substantial control over project planning and execution, and that delegation will be a slow process, which is understandable in view of the need to build up domestic capacity. An important related feature is that there will be only one single budget and that the project will be executed according to normal domestic procedures. Separate accounts of the project must be kept, and the accounts will be audited by the audit department of the Government, or any other entity designated with the agreement of the UNDP.

During the first decade of pre-investment activity, the principal sources of follow-up financing were 40% domestic, 36% multilateral, 18% official bilateral and 6% private bilateral. Capacity for financial and economic analysis within the UN Specialised Agencies has since improved and is now complemented by the existing World Bank cooperative programmes with a number of these agencies. The multilateral system seems well placed to meet the qualitative needs of the less industrialised countries for pre-investment projects prepared for immediate follow-up investments.

Ideally the developing country government, once pre-investment work is completed, should be in a position to select the source and type of finance from the countries and agencies with which it prefers to deal. However, experience shows that it is difficult to make this separation between pre-investment work and the subsequent lender and development partner. While it is possible to disconnect certain types of pre-investment surveys (for example, resource and sector surveys) from the source of future lending, this is not as easy when work has advanced through the feasibility stage. And since most external resources are still provided on a bilateral basis, most feasibility studies and other pre-investment work will continue to be done on a bilateral basis.

It will therefore be in the interest of the developing countries to become increasingly and decisively involved in the field of pre-investment. This is particularly significant in such areas as mineral and other natural resource surveys, where the potential influence of private and official bilateral involvement is particularly strong.

With the introduction of the system of country programming as a result of the Capacity Study, the separate function of pre-investment was transferred to the UNDP. Pre-investment projects became part of the country programming exercise based on Government priorities and an indicative planning figure. This meant that the domestic government could be persuaded by the respective interested parties, including the World Bank, the regional development banks and the Specialised Agencies, to include pre-investment work in the country programme of a type that lends itself to specific follow-up investment. An Investment Follow-up Division was established in the UNDP for the purpose of promoting inter-disciplinary integration in programme and project planning with special reference to opportunities and requirements for investments. It worked out guidelines for officers at headquarters and in the field offices to increase the volume and improve the design and execution of investment-oriented projects.

Nonetheless coordination and integration within the UN system is not a simple matter, and the problem of satisfying conflicting demands for flexibility, speed and care in project design and execution remains. We seem to be caught in a dilemma: as the need for aid increases, the growth of the UN system itself becomes a problem. While the challenge of development increases in magnitude, the capacity and willingness to respond to it wavers, partly because the transfer of resources cannot be adequatly managed by the recipients. In essence, the problem is one of control and of unclearly perceived conflicts of interest.

## C. The World Bank

When examining problems of institution-building and project appraisal, discussed in general terms in Chapter Two, it is useful to look at the work of the World Bank for several reasons. Since it has funds to dispense at what many consider an attractive interest rate, it has leverage and can strongly influence patterns of development. Secondly, it uses project-appraisal techniques widely for its project funding and indeed by virtue of its statutes is compelled to do so. Third, it has an Operations Evaluation Department (OED) that produces project-performance audits which can provide valuable feedback for on-going appraisals. Fourth, and more tangibly, it has become the most influential bilateral agency, combining the functions of a bank with those of a development institution.

The World Bank lends only for specific projects, "except in special circumstances" (4). The emphasis on volume in project lending has contributed to the establishment of institutions designed primarily to absorb specific types of development loans and credits. However, basic institution-building takes time and the World Bank cannot be expected to supply more than a fraction of the technical assistance required.

The growth of the work of the Bank has been impressive. In 1968 it decided to double global lending, to triple lending to Africa, to double lending to Latin-America, to quadruple lending for agriculture, and to triple lending for education, all during the following five years. These targets were all met and surpassed (5). As early as 1965 the Bank established missions in Eastern and Western Africa, partly to help produce bankable projects. This was in the interest of the borrower as well as the Bank but it necessitated a Bank policy decision of considerable consequence: in order to secure a pipeline of projects, the Bank actively engaged itself in the identification and preparation of projects which were later to be submitted to the Bank for its own appraisal. Methodologically this was recognised as unsound, but for practical purposes it was regarded as inevitable. The pressure for volume also led the Bank to finance some of the work of FAO, UNESCO, and WHO to secure the required supply of investment projects.

### 1. Project-Appraisal Techniques and the World Bank

The World Bank uses a cost-benefit methodology in the form of a rate of return analysis on as many projects as possible. However in "soft sectors", such as health and population planning, efforts to quantify benefits have been dropped.

Technical departments have traditionally been strong. Research is carried out to guide project identification; for example, a study on road construction will include special references to employment generation and energy consumption. Volume targets nonetheless constitute a constraint: alternatives to existing solutions are often time consuming and involve great risks, one of them being the risk of missing the volume target.

The benefit of using the Bank's method of project analysis should be judged in relation to its cost. The cost to the Bank has been estimated, and appraisal work constitutes the most important single element. Unit costs have risen steadily, partly as a result of changed geographical and sectoral emphasis, and partly because qualitative improvements absorb additional staff time.

We cannot estimate the opportunity cost to the borrower of time spent by scarce domestic staff in the process, but there is no doubt that it is high. World Bank missions are frequent, and contacts are usually at a high level. Other external missions make similar demands.

## 2. Project Appraisal in "Hard" and "Soft" Sectors

Robert McNamara's speech at Nairobi in September 1973 constituted a turning point for the World Bank: lending moved increasingly towards the "soft" sectors, with emphasis on poverty, rural development and "social" projects.

This trend affects pre-investment work in several ways. Surveys, pre-feasibility studies and project preparation have become considerably more complex, and data are harder to get. Sectors and subsectors overlap and have to be integrated, and there are comparatively fewer foreign consultants with experience in the relevant fields. This means that the World Bank has increasingly had to rely on its own efforts for the pre-investment work necessary to produce bankable projects, although cooperation with the UN Specialised Agencies has also been expanded.

The Bank has traditionally been equipped to finance projects in hard infrastructure, where the contours and limits of the project itself have been sharper and relevant institution-building simpler. Work in education and rural development is considerably more complex and necessitates a broader coverage; World Bank projects are already programmes in practice in these fields.

The shift in emphasis in sectoral allocation has implications for induced institutional development in developing countries. Investments in hard infrastructure, like transport, power and communications, have been made largely through independent agencies which

the Bank has helped to achieve financial viability. This aspect of
revenue generation has made domestic agencies strong in their own
right; the Bank, having funds as well as technical advice, has
developed into an influential development agency. However the gestation period of "soft" projects is long and the returns uncertain.
It will take a long time to find out whether the Bank's investment
in agriculture and education can develop strong domestic institutions in the manner of the "hard" sector. Important factors are as
always domestic politics as well as management and complementary
support from the external agencies.

### 3. World Bank Relationships with Multilateral and Bilateral Agencies in Pre-investment Work

The Bank has lacked expertise in certain areas and has had to become
more like a technical assistance agency than was previously the case.
The relationship of the Bank to the UN agencies has been considered
by Mason and Asher in their book on World Bank operations (6).

They have drawn attention to what they call the mystique of pre-
investment, resulting from the assignment of this function to one
autonomous agency within the United Nations (7) and of separating
the function of project planning into pre-investment and investment
agencies, an administrative split which is further aggravated by a
tendency to perpetuate the arbitrary division between grants and
loans (8). The fact that UNDP and the World Bank have different
memberships, policies, and administrative practices (9) does not
make the matter less complicated.

The World Bank is still an important source of follow-up investment
for the UNDP. This is in the interest both of UNDP and the World
Bank, and the Bank makes the best possible use of existing opportunities within the UN system to stimulate the production of bankable
projects. This primarily takes the form of close cooperation with
the Specialised Agencies, which produce projects with Bank assistance for later joint financing.

It is an open question what the World Bank mode of operation has
meant for the UN Specialised Agencies with which it collaborates.
Even though there is bound to be an influence in both directions,
with the Bank becoming familiar with the pros and cons of using
individual experts (in-house or hired) as is normally done by the
FAO, UNESCO and WHO, it seems likely that the practice of the World
Bank will make a relatively stronger impact on the Specialised
Agencies.

## 4. Institution-building and the World Bank

World Bank efforts at basic institution-building have centred around
the activities and technical assistance of the Planning Advisory
Division of the International Relations Department. This type of
work is difficult and requires competent and devoted people who are
hard to find. Widespread transfer of the necessary skills is a
major undertaking.

A case in point is Brazil. In the early Sixties, the World Bank
began to provide a series of loans for highway, railroad and port
projects. For some ten years, effective cooperation was maintained
between Brazilian engineers and planners, World Bank staff and
other experts. As a result, the Brazilian transport sector and related agencies became strong, and the consulting and construction industries grew to international stature. This illustrates two important
points. First, sectoral allocations and project lending can increase
domestic  capacity in that sector, and the power to attract domestic and external funds increases correspondingly. Second, it highlights the important role the World Bank can play in institution-
building.

There seems to be growing recognition within the Bank that in lieu
of elite units for individual projects and agencies, what is needed
is a central institution capable of handling the selection and elaboration of projects in all sectors in order to verify whether they
are "bankable". A definition of a bankable project can be one which,
according to professional appraisal, promises internal financial and
economic returns of a certain size. Hence the need for closer integration of the UN system to make more functional mixes of capital and
technical assistance possible.

The cutting edge of the World Bank approach is its insistence on
quality at the project level: it can ask for a minimum of quality
in organization, accounting, project appraisal and supervision. The
World Bank supports a training programme through its Economic Development Institute. It also helps to build up sectoral capability
and offers technical-assistance loans to a number of countries which
can be used, with or without a central pre-investment framework, for
consultancy services in project planning and preparation.

As more and more of the poorer and less developed countries became
members, the Bank recognised the need for a project preparation
facility which it set up in late 1975. It realized that project
preparation was a time-consuming and expensive use of Bank staff,
but only a few resident missions had project preparation capabilities,
and excessive involvement of Bank staff in preparation might make

the host government feel that the project was not its own but the Bank's. Since UNDP could not provide the necessary resources on a grant basis, it was decided that the World Bank would advance the necessary funds.

This shows that the Bank responds pragmatically and flexibly to needs connected with project lending. Project preparation is expensive, especially since much of it must be done by foreign consultants and experts, and developing countries are often reluctant to allocate scarce foreign exchange for the purpose. It also shows that the international system of development cooperation is deficient as far as institution-building for projects is concerned. Few bilateral agencies have paid attention to this need.

# CHAPTER V

## DEVELOPING PROJECT INSTITUTIONS IN A SOFT SECTOR: RURAL DEVELOPMENT

### I. The Special Nature of Rural Development Projects

We have shown that greater capacity for identifying and appraising projects lies in the hard sectors, because they are easier to appraise and have a tangible stream of benefits flowing from a known point in time. As a result scarce manpower tends to concentrate here, and more projects are generated. Donors and lenders have been willing to fund projects which have proved successful and comparatively simple to design. The pressure on lenders to disburse funds and on borrowers to repay loans is also part of the explanation. Many borrowers have quotas with major multilateral banks and are unwilling to see part of them used for projects where the magnitude and timing of benefits are uncertain. The emphasis on hard sector projects has contributed to high rates of economic growth, but benefits have not reached the mass of rural poor. Rural development projects require changes in technology, new institutions and mass participation. The new strategy has been described under several different names such as "Poverty Focussed Planning" and "Provision of Basic Needs". We shall not enter the debate except to say that no country can ignore generating productive capacity among the large majority of its population for very long without serious economic and political consequences.

Promoting "new style" rural development is much more complex than investing in "old-style" agricultural production projects. It involves carrying out new research and developing new techniques and institutions. Rural development has been defined by Uma Lele as improving "living standards of the mass of the low-income population residing in rural areas and making the process of their development self-sustaining" (1). She describes three important features which should determine how rural development programs are designed and implemented.

1) "Improving the living standards of the subsistence population involves mobilisation and allocation of resources so as to reach a desirable balance over time between the welfare and productive services available to the subsistence rural sectors".

2) "Mass participation requires that resources be allocated to low-income regions and classes and that the productive and social services actually reach them".

3) "Making the process self-sustaining requires development of
   the appropriate skills and implementing capacity and the presence of institutions at the local and national levels to ensure  the effective use of existing resources and to foster
   the mobilisation of additional financial and human resources
   for continued development of the subsistence sector. Self-
   sustenance thus means involving, as distinct from simply reach-
   ing, the subsistence population through development programs"
   (2).

It must be admitted that the predictive power for bringing about
successful rural development is very limited at present and the hard
pressed project officer, who already finds implementing "old" agricultural projects fraught with the usual difficulties such as obtaining inputs on time, training staff and overcoming natural disasters,
is now being instructed to expand the number and range of beneficiaries by "finer tuning", even to the point, for projects such as
those in nutrition, of recognising the differential access to resources within families. The implications of the new rural development
or basic needs strategy for project design may seem intimidating.
Nevertheless there exists considerable unused capacity even among
the poorest people in society, and momentum, adaptation, institution-building and incentives can be developed by the beneficiaries
themselves.

The problems involved in the improvement of nutrition illustrate
the situation, for it is an important objective of most rural development projects. The selection of projects that can fulfil this
objective involves many of the problems that we have so far discussed i.e. dependence on Western technology and experts, conflicts
of interest in domestic planning agencies, uncertainty in predicting
outcomes from inputs, and a lack of suitable appraisal criteria
manageable within institutional structures.

Nutrition-related projects are of two main types: traditional nutrition projects aimed at direct improvement, for example, feeding programmes of various sorts, fortification of foods, and development of
special foods; second, projects in other sectors have an impact on
nutrition, positive or negative. As well as investment in health,
agriculture, education and employment generation, projects such as
road building can bring about dietary change. Indeed if problems
of nutrition are to be solved, other sectors must be made aware of
them.

Dependence on Western technology and ideas has been manifest in past
attempts to solve nutrition problems. For example, much effort was
expended, for example, on low-cost weaning food; however, it reached

only a small proportion of the population, and those it did reach could not afford it, did not like it, and did not think it necessary. Other nutrition approaches have foundered because they have been based on the belief that intervention in the market place can solve nutrition problems.

In most countries nutrition problems are handled by special units in Ministries of Health, Agriculture, and sometimes Education. Some parastatals are also involved, as well as voluntary agencies. Co-ordination is rare but, more important, there is not much direct financing for nutrition: for example, a tractorisation project reduces employment and may, despite increased aggregate agricultural production, have an adverse effect on nutrition. This again raises the problem of who should be responsible for projects covered by several ministries. The usual response is to create a new Ministry or to set up a special unit in the office of the Prime Minister or President. However, this is rarely successful.

Uncertain results present the biggest problem in selecting nutrition projects, and it is difficult to generalize about how nutrition (intake and status) might change in response to a certain project or policy. It cannot be assumed that most forms of economic development will improve nutrition quickly enough. But we do know that when designing nutrition projects, attention must be paid to the differential access to resources within families in view of research and evaluation of previous projects. Ideally, the institution responsible for design should also be responsible for monitoring, evaluation and new design. However, as we have seen, existing project institutions do not even have adequate capacity to appraise all projects. The suggestion for an agency involved in all stages of the project cycle is not new (3), but pressures for rural development may bring it about.

## II. Identification of Rural Development Projects

Rural development projects have become very popular with donors; virtually all bilateral and multilateral agencies have issued statements and policy guidelines to the effect that their aid shall be concentrated on improving the welfare of the large numbers of rural poor. The International Fund for Agricultural Development (IFAD) was created expressly to provide finance for the rural poor. Bilaterals responded in this way not only because they were aware that the rural poor are a major problem in developing countries but also because public opinion does not want aid to go to urban or rural elites. As a result there were more funds than projects in the Seventies (4). Most countries were visited by missions with instructions to commit large amounts of money in this field or to find ideas for investment and institutions with whom to cooperate. But so far rural development projects are not very different in design from the agriculture projects of the past.

Visiting missions carrying out sector surveys talk to experts and politicians in the country, who make recommendations based on what they know to be politically expedient, technically possible and least socially disruptive. However, for a project to promote rural development, recommendations must come from many sources, for the rural sector cuts across several functional ministries. If a rural development project covers, for example, improved seeds for food crops to increase production, clinics to provide basic health care and an adult literacy programme, then three Ministries - Agriculture Health and Education - are involved. Communication among them may be facilitated at the identification stage by the participation of aid agencies. The World Bank is closely involved with countries at the project-identification stage through its sector surveys, one function of which is to generate projects (5).

Team work is indispensible because of the bias of individual disciplines and perceptions. Officials, indigenous as well as expatriate, are usually trained along Western lines, a training which does not encourage them (in fact positively discourages them) to consider elements of a project outside their specialisation. An economist will tend to disregard the importance of social relations, while a rural sociologist will pay lip service to the importance of financial incentives.

III. Preparation of Rural Development Projects

We have not compared the time required to prepare rural development projects with that of agricultural projects. We know that the World Bank's recent nutrition projects have taken more than average time, but this was to be expected in view of the innovative aspects involved. With identical investment volumes, the preparation phase of a rural development project (indeed the whole project cycle) should take longer than that of an agricultural project given its greater complexity and uncertainty (6). A major theme of this study is the inadequacy of institutions to integrate project selection. In rural development this is crucial, and here target groups rather than rates of return should be the main focus. A rural development project can be stifled if each institution does its own work without considering the others involved. This means that bureaucracy must be reduced, preparation must not be excessive, and implementation must confirm and guide preparation in a collective effort to learn by doing. It also means that overall management and co-ordination is of special importance.

Institutions involved in rural development often have to use inappropriate technology. For example, most of the research in crop production has been developed with income generation per se in mind; prosperous farmers tend to be favoured by improved crop varieties for they require capital investment and purchased inputs (e.g. fertilisers, irrigation water) which the poorer farmers cannot afford. Although the situation is changing, improved technology for the rural poor - improved varieties of such inferior grains as millets and sorghums, and of cassava, easier ways of carrying water, reduced drudgery of hand labour on and off the farm - has not yet been developed. Therefore institutions based on foreign models often transplant Western technology into an inappropriate setting.

## IV. Appraisal of Rural Development Projects

Conventional appraisal criteria (cost-benefit ratio, rate of return) have to be modified for "soft" sectors in view of the high proportion of unquantifiable benefits. In theory, of course, it is possible to attach a benefit figure to improved health, decreased mortality or morbidity but such calculations are not very meaningful. Also a shadow price for labour may result in an inacceptably low benefit figure for a life saved.

Therefore, other appraisal criteria such as cost effectiveness must be used. The synergistic effects of different efforts should also be explored, e.g. the physical and technical infrastructure required to install a network of clinics might be the same as a water supply network. And the clinics might be integrated into a farm service centre which sells improved seeds and fertiliser, thereby reducing cost. The unit responsible for appraisal must be independent and instructed to estimate the effects of all components and their interaction. Comparison among alternatives is still uncommon. One reason for this is the shortage of prepared projects. Comparison of alternative design is also hampered by overall deadlines and the time required for different components.

Some important aspects of project selection in rural development have been discussed by Chambers (7). He believes that present planning techniques are too complicated and stresses the need for simplicity. Donors want projects which are large, capital and import intensive rather than administration intensive, easy to monitor, quick to implement (with foreign skills if necessary) and suitable for social cost-benefit analysis (8). Big projects are bankable, have a high import content and are therefore politically acceptable. Limited administrative capacity (at home and abroad) is a convenient excuse. Chambers confirms our observation that the decision to fund

a project can come well before formal appraisal. To improve project
selection and increase mobilisation for poverty-focussed rural development, Chambers recommends simplifying procedures: decentralisation and greater financial discretion for staff at the local level,
and use of appraisal criteria other than cost-benefit analysis,
such as decision matrices, poverty-group rankings, checklists and
cost-effectiveness.

V. Improvement of Project Management in Rural Development

We shall now review two approaches to improve project management and
their relation to project selection: Chambers' work on managing
rural development (9), which includes the Programming and Implementation (PIM) system, and Imboden's work on a management approach to
project appraisal and evaluation (10).

It is worth noting that the work of Kulp (11), a comprehensive
application of systems analysis to rural development, is concerned
with project implementation rather than project choice. His discussion of project appraisal is confined to conventional statements
about costs and benefits (12). The same applies to shadow pricing
(13). He does not discuss alternative means of appraisal. He presents
case studies of planning in Senegal, Bangladesh, Malaysia and Taiwan,
and although individual cases vary, project selection is carried out
largely on the basis of a principle enunciated in the early part of
the book (14):

> "It (the commune or village organisation) has an annual budget
> which may allocate to a variety of infrastructure projects of
> its own choosing".

In general it appears that Kulp is advocating no formal appraisal
as such for projects generated at the local level. His apparent
neglect of project-selection methods is similar to Chambers' de-
emphasis of formal appraisal criteria. It is implied that if projects are initiated "bottom-up" by the participants themselves
(rather than "top-down" by government or district officials), measu-
rement of profitability is less important since needs have been expressed by the intended beneficiaries.

A. The P.I.M. System

The PIM system covers all stages of the project cycle, but we inclu-
de it here as an interesting example of institutional innovation.
The system, which has been used in the context of the Special Rural
Development Programme (SRDP) in Kenya, has three basic components:

> "a programming exercise, which in the SRDP was annual and held
> just before or after the beginning of the financial year. This

is a meeting attended by all those directly concerned with implementation at which they jointly and freely draw up a phased
programme for the year;

a management meeting, which in the SRDP was usually monthly.
At this meeting attended by those concerned directly with implementation, progress is reviewed against the phased work programme, bottlenecks are identified, and remedial action agreed upon;

an action report which in the SRDP was described as a monthly
management report, summarising briefly the progress made and
problems encountered, naming those responsible for action, and
sent quickly and simultaneously to those concerned at different
levels in government" (15).

Some of the principles incorporated in the PIM system are:
- "a procedure requiring joint programming by all those responsible for implementation;
- a staff taking part in setting their own work targets;
- collegial sanctions against poor work;
- lean and functional reports;
- communication direct from the implementor to the point of
  bottleneck or delay;
- functional meetings used sparingly;
- sophistication in simplicity" (16).

Given our emphasis on project selection, we are more concerned with
the Programming Exercise. For any project this involves agreeing on
what has to be done, who should do it and the timing of operations.
Projects selected for programming have high national priority, a
large resource input, and require collaboration of large numbers of
staff. "For each project in turn, the action co-ordinator invites
those staff members directly, concerned with implementation to a
joint programming meeting which is held either just before or just
after the start of the financial year. The person from headquarters
who is responsible for the necessary fund releases also attends.
Those present may be from one or more ministries and departments,
and from one or more levels in the hierarchy" (17).

In this meeting the objectives and design of the project are discussed. Then in an open discussion the various stages, responsibilities,
targets and timing are agreed upon. Thus communication is maximised
within all sections of project administration, and each participant
is aware of what has been agreed in a non-authoritarian atmosphere.

We are not recommending that this sort of open discussion should
replace project selection and the quantification of costs and benefits, for the experience of the SRDPs was a very special one.

The areas chosen were designated for innovative types of rural development with individual bilateral donors (ODA, NORAD, SIDA, USAID) supporting an area each. However, we suggest that in view of the scant institutional resources for project selection in most sectors (even in "hard" sectors not all projects get appraised) as well as the extra institutional demands of multisectoral rural development work (inter-ministerial cooperation, greater detail in response to greater uncertainty, generating local participation), a system such as PIM might be used to good effect.

B. A Management Approach to Project Appraisal and Evaluation

A major theme in Imboden's work is that project appraisal and evaluation can become a management tool for decision-making within a project, and he shows how evaluations can be integrated into the management system. The concept for a project cycle with distinct steps and corresponding institutional arrangements is less valid for rural development projects. He recognises the importance of the institutional factor, however, and the need for simplicity:

> "It is contended that most methodologies proposed are not taking into account the institutional and organisational aspects of the countries concerned and often misjudge the decision-making structure. The methods are analytically complex and are too demanding in terms of data and planning capacity. They do not take into account the realities of staffing, time pressure and data availability in less developed countries" (18).

The emphasis of these methodologies is on prediction rather than on problem identification and solving. Imboden has developed an iterative-impact approach which goes beyond the traditional estimation of costs and benefits to monitor social policy and decision-making in general. It requires "that the feedback from project evaluation to planning analysis be institutionalised" (19). To make this work, a sophisticated administrative system must be set up at the very beginning of the project, and there must be high-level support so that project managers do not feel threatened. Management is held responsible for achievement of project objectives; staff, whose sole responsibility is evaluation, works closely with the decision-making level which uses the information. A combination of outside investigation (i.e. consultants) and in-house monitoring is necessary.

VI. Concluding Comments: Project Institution in "Soft" Sectors

It is clear that the softer the project, the softer the project cycle, and that rural development projects must have internal feedback mechanisms as well as feedback for the next project. This is now increasingly recognised, as shown by the work of Chambers, Imboden and also of Heimpel.

> "It should be noted that planning for an agricultural project is always done with scarce information, since the required data and particulars for devising 'good ideas' and for formulating quantitative part-plans do not usually become available until implementation of the project is in progress" (20).

Therefore planning and review should be continuous, and as far as possible participants should be involved in the whole process. Rural development projects require much attention to mobilisation, participation, organisation and management as well as to power relations. Oversophisticated appraisal techniques and overemphasis on quantification will hinder rather than help the development process. Though assistance is needed more than ever, there is a definite limit to how much an outsider can understand and even facilitate.

CHAPTER VI

DEVELOPING DOMESTIC CAPACITY: THE ROLE OF CONSULTANTS

At several points we have emphasised the importance of consultants
in project selection, and the positive and negative effects they
can have on domestic capacity. We will now see how consultants are
related to the three stages of the project cycle, that is, identification, preparation and appraisal, and how they could be better
used in domestic systems.

In the developing countries, where external financing and/or assistance is necessary, most of the work in project feasibility, design
and implementation is done by foreign consultants and contractors.
Though the borrower, lender or donor is the principal or joint
contracting agency and administrator, the actual work of project
preparation and the transfer of technology is done by individual
consultants and experts, consulting firms, suppliers of equipment
and construction firms. Developing countries must depend to a large
extent on external judgments and concepts for solutions and
institution-building.

International agencies like the World Bank and the regional banks
play an important role in setting standards and designing procedures
for domestic and foreign consultants, which enables recipient governments to increase their control over, and improve the administration
of technology transfer. Competitive international bidding on studies
and project design based on accepted procedures guarantees quality,
which makes the cost of the studies a secondary factor. While the
advantages of such a system are obvious, the disadvantages can also
be great: since domestic consultants are usually not strong enough
to compete with foreign consultants, the state of dependency conti-
nues while the desire for self-reliance grows.

I. Types of Consultants

The term "consultant" is very broad: it can refer to an individual
or a firm, and to almost any type of activity. Consultants are now
called upon for short or long periods of time for all kinds of
problem-solving. The top management of a public or private enterprise
can today select almost any function within its organization and
decide that it will be performed by an outside expert or organization.
This offers great flexibility and opportunities for renewal.

Broadly speaking, there are three main categories of consultants
working in the developing countries: technical, management and

economic consultants. In highly simplified terms, technical consultants give advice on what to do, management consultants on how to do it, and economic consultants on costs and benefits. Consultants can potentially be used for every aspect of a national development effort, and there is a high degree of specialization. Most of the big contracts in development cooperation go to engineering and project management firms.

Depending on the services needed, the client decides to hire an individual consultant or expert, or a consulting firm. Generally speaking, individuals are hired to bolster staff resources, while firms are called upon to solve specific, difficult problems. However, the consulting industry has developed in such a way that certain professions are found in firms. For example, engineering consultants generally operate within firms, while physicians and agricultural experts often act alone. Some firms try to provide a complete range of services, others may subcontract a particular expertise, while still others specialize in a narrow field like quantity surveying in construction.

When choosing consultants, questions of continuity and speed are important. It usually takes longer to recruit individual consultants, and they may not be available for follow-up assignments. A firm generally acts faster, offers backstopping and continuity of service, and takes responsibility for the work done. On the other hand, individual experts may sometimes show greater independence of judgment and freedom from vested interests. The best solution for the client depends on the complexity of the assignment and the domestic capacity for administration and supervision.

Management Consulting. Management is a key issue in development everywhere and it can prove to be the most difficult of all skills to transfer. Construction techniques can be used in much the same way anywhere. Similarly, economic analysis can be carried out by applying standard principles, constrained only by the lack of data. But management depends upon the entire cultural, social, economic and political context. It is not surprising therefore that management consultancy meets with more varying degrees of success than, say, engineering. Although management consulting began in the private sector of free-market economies, it is now in great demand in the public sector in both socialist and capitalist countries.

Since implementation is admittedly more difficult than planning, there is a strong case for involving management consultants in the early stages of planning, for it is impossible to implement well that which has been poorly planned. However, management consultants have been known to duplicate systems that look beautiful on paper but that are difficult to apply in a different context. Selection of management consultants is therefore crucial. They will be useful only to the extent that they understand local conditions fully - an important argument for developing a competent corps of domestic management consultants.

The main areas of management consulting are finance, marketing, production and personnel management, information systems and data processing. Management consultants may also find themselves confronted with politically sensitive issues and, like other consultants, they should be prepared to make unpopular recommendations. On the other hand, it may be useless for a consultant to present a report that is clearly unacceptable politically.

In recent years, their services have been in growing demand, especially in countries with enough foreign exchange (notably the oil producers) and absorptive capacity. Though management consulting services are one step removed from the investment as such, their cost adds considerably to the total foreign consultancy bill. But their recommendations are as a rule impartial since they have no ties with export interests. The real challenge they face is to design appropriate systems for an alien milieu.

## II. Types of Assignment

Consultancy work at various stages of the project cycle (reconnaissance, pre-feasibility or feasibility studies) differs in nature and depth and requires different terms of reference. The integrated approach to development increasingly taken by host governments and external agencies makes great demands on conception and utilisation of required consultant services and the definition of responsibilities of principal parties, notably the client, the foreign investor or lender, the contractor, the foreign and domestic consultants. In many cases a relevant study has already been done and should be updated rather than repeated at great expense. Most developing countries would profit from some research on existing studies and reports before commissioning new ones. But without an inventory, time often does not allow for such research.

Turn-key and project management. Two common solutions for project planning and implementation that influence the choice of consultants are the turn-key project and project management. In a turn-key project, the client leaves the whole process of feasibility, design, procurement and construction up to the enterprise, usually in the manufacturing industry. The client has only to "turn the key" to open up his new establishment. This is very different from the

conventional systems in which design and specifications are prepared
by a consultant or an engineer, and the contractor does the rest.

The advantage of a turn-key plant is its simplicity and speedy planning and implementation. It is commonly used for industrial projects
financed on commercial terms, the aim being to get into production
quickly. Since the domestic government or agency has to deal with
only one contractor, it can obtain guarantees on time schedules,
project performance and costs. Working relations are simplified and
delays reduced. However, as the client has only limited control over
the planning and implementation process, he should pay great attention to the details of the contract. The proposed solution may not
be the most appropriate; bidding procedures may be unclear or left
unstipulated; and cost comparisons cannot always be made. Unless
the client continuously reviews progress with the contractor, he
may  not know the real value of the project until it is in operation.

For these reasons, the turn-key approach is most suitable for fairly
straightforward projects which use a limited number of processes and
which have a clearly defined cost ceiling. For the client, the most
important thing is to negotiate capacity or assistance for the
entire contract and effective monitoring arrangements. Here consultant services may substantially improve the end result of turn-key
plants.

For large and complex projects the project management approach is
more usual. The normal procedure is to engage a consulting firm to
manage the individual contracts and sub-contracts. The responsibilities of the consulting firm thus include pre-feasibility, feasibility, design, procurement, construction, supervision, and execution in the management of multiple contracts. An important aspect
of these multiple contracts is training, what is called commissioning, which includes the preparation of manuals for operation,
safety, maintenance, recruitment and training, operating checks,
trial runs and performance tests, at which point the client takes
over.

The management of complex contracts requires considerable experience
and imagination  and knowledge of local conditions and constraints.
It is equally important that the basic contract be clearly defined,
so that it becomes an effective instrument for planning and implementation. This refers particularly to the place of the consultant
firm in the consortium, which is usually formed for the purpose,
and its authority and responsibility as agent for the client. If the
firm is a full member of the consortium, it can then act as leader
and coordinator, accepting overall responsibility and risks. However,
it would have to be completely independent of third-party interests.

The main advantage of the project management method is that it allows for a more tailor-made approach to the project complex, including costs. The consulting firm, on behalf of the client, can secure the most appropriate solution in each specific case, and contracts for each component - construction, supplies or training - can be awarded on the basis of competitive bidding. In other words, expert advice is available at all stages of the project and sufficient flexibility exists to make the required changes. Maximum use of local experts, consultants, and contractors can be made, costs can be better controlled, and monitoring more effectively secured. On the other hand, it may be hard to establish a cost ceiling, and it is usually impossible for the consultant firm to guarantee the performance of the installation or the completion date.

III. Selection of Consultants

Ways of selecting consultants vary widely in the developing countries, and as clients lack experience in formulating enquiries, the consultant may discover that the job is different from what had been outlined. Some consistency does exist however: multilateral agencies use similar procedures, up to and including international competitive bidding. Bilateral agencies tie selection to the use of their own nationals, both for practical and policy reasons. Bilateral donors and lenders prefer to use their own consultants to protect their commercial interests. In some countries, this is mandatory but it also makes sense: since a developing country usually wants specific knowledge and technology transfer, it wants assistance from a particular developed country. However bilaterals sometimes go beyond their own borders when they lack a particular expertise or when they want to promote technology transfer from one developing country to another.

Sometimes selection can be wasteful: too many consultants are invited to present proposals, and consistent rules would benefit all parties, particularly the client.

Selecting consultants is more or less difficult, depending on the complexity of the project. Complex projects usually require multi-disciplinary teams and a phased approach. Special advice is necessary to select both the team and the team-leader. It may be worthwhile to let a single firm handle the entire project, or different assignments may sometimes require a number of different consultants or teams. In multi-disciplinary teams, there may be conflicting interests: an engineering firm, for example, has the necessary technology at hand and can get the job done quickly, but the team economist raises questions about economic feasibility and the sociologist examines the social impact of the project. All this can prove irksome to the engineer.

## A. Price Variations

Arbitration between price and quality depends to a great
extent on the type of project. For projects with standardised methodology, such as the design of straightforward railway or port projects, conventional power stations or ground water surveys, price
is an important factor. But for projects at the feasibility stage,
the development of methodology for data gathering and studies may
involve a range of social, cultural, environmental, management,
institutional and legal factors. Here the quality of the proposal
is more important than the price. This is equally true of highly
complex projects at the design stage, where volume, risks and benefits are great enough to make the price of the consultant much less
important than quality.

There are many arguments against prices proposals: to get a contract,
a firm may in fact be offering second-rate staff; the best firms
may be unwilling to compete on a price basis since this may jeopar-
dise their reputation for quality; and, last, a maximum price may
tempt the consultant to design the proposal to meet the ceiling
established.

Even when proposals are judged primarily on the basis of quality,
the choice can be arbitrary unless some simple, consistent system
of evaluation is used. The most common procedure is to evaluate
proposals by looking at the firm's experience, its general approach
to the problem and the specific plan of study, and the quality of
the staff to be assigned. These aspects can then be weighted according to the specific assignment: for example, the quality of the
staff is particularly important for engineering and supervision work,
while a firm's experience is particularly relevant at the pre-
feasibility stage.

Bids may be priced or unpriced; each approach presents advantages
and disadvantages. A firm chosen for its quality has a distinct
advantage in the ensuing price negotiations. The firm knows that it
has been judged outstanding and may take advantage of the fact;
moreover, the client will find it distinctly inconvenient if price
negotiations fail, for he will lose time over a new round of negotiations with another bidder.

## B. A Framework for Selection of Consultants

An interesting example of the use of consultants for repeated
assignments under a general contract is USAID's special arrangement
called Indefinite Quantity Contracts (IQC), which has been in operation for some years. AID rules prescribe that every project be

evaluated once a year on the basis of guidelines designed for the purpose. In order to shorten recruitment time which normally took from two to three months, AID selected a stable of consultant firms specialized in economics and the social sciences to work closely with its Headquarters, field missions and host governments. They were guaranteed a minimum annual fee and could be brought into the field within two to three weeks.

AID organized seminars to train IQC consultants in project design and evaluation, AID policy, procedures and methods. They were then at the disposal of the field missions and the host government. The IQC consultants collaborated as much as possible with local experts, including university staff and could sub-contract locally.

IV. Terms of Reference

Terms of reference are at the heart of consultancy, dictating what is to be done, when, and by whom. Bad terms of reference will almost invariably lead to a bad job, unless a client and a consultant of exceptional talent happen to be working together. Indeed, the greatest advance in the field of consultancy may come about through better preparation of the terms of reference. It is essential that they address themselves to the real problems and possibilities. Too often assumptions are made at an early stage on inadequate data; sometimes, despite protracted discussions, the terms of reference are too ambitious, exclusive or limited. Terms of reference for design and construction projects are different from those of a regional development project. They are also easier to draft. Decisions taken during the pre-feasibility and feasibility stages are the most important, and therefore adequate terms of reference for studies prior to such decisions are essential. Those drafted for consultants by the client or the financer should be well thought out and comprehensive but never so firm as to prevent a bidder from proposing alternatives. In fact, agencies and clients which give the consultant credit for critical appraisal of the terms of reference probably get better bids and better jobs in consequence. Many consultants, on the other hand, avoid commenting critically on the terms of reference for fear of losing the contract.

A. The Phased Approach

For all complex projects the terms of reference should allow for a phased approach. Segments of work should lead to decision points for the client, and on these decisions the next segments should depend. Besides preventing or reducing waste, this also has the advantage of carrying the client along with the emerging

conclusions and avoiding major confrontation on points of principle
at a later stage when most of the resources have been utilised.
However, a phased approach is not necessarily cheaper, if a multi-
disciplinary team produces a piece of work and must then wait for
a decision, several field trips will be necessary. But experience
shows that the results will more than repay any immediate additional
costs. There should always be provision for changes of direction in
the course of any study, whatever the terms of reference. They
should merely be a guide, formulated at the beginning of an assignment, and when new factors emerge, as they often do, they should not
be ignored (as they unfortunately often are).

The phased assignment with clear decision points established along
the way also makes it easier to deal with sensitive problems and
unpopular findings in time. Phased assignments with interim report-
ing also enable the sub-contractors to gain access to the client,
which can be difficult when there is only one consultant firm or
when the sub-contractor differs with the main contractor.

The phased approach may involve a test operation on a limited scale
in order to gain experience for further planning. For example, during
the process of planning for a rural development project, a small
team of experts can run certain extension, credit and marketing services in cooperation with host government staff. The findings during
this "plan as you work" period can then be used for planning the final
project. The need to define the problem and to consider alternative
developments, projects and design usually requires multidisciplinary
teams at the early stages, and raises the questions of team composition
and leadership and responsibility for the terms of reference.

B. Multidisciplinary teams

    For large and complex projects, terms of reference should be
drawn up by representatives of all the disciplines involved. Leadership of the multidisciplinary team is often given to the person or
firm that is most involved in the project, although there is no
reason why leadership should not change as the project progresses
through various stages. The important factor is the ability to lead
and to create a good working team, regardless of the discipline of
the leader. The composition of the team will depend on the size and
the nature of the project. It is simpler to build a bridge than to
develop a rural area. However, for all projects there is a case for
involving economists and management consultants from the start. To
define the problem, a reconnaissance visit to the area, before the
terms of reference are drafted, may be necessary.

## V. The Costs and Effectiveness of Consultant Studies

Value for money is a more important consideration than cost as such. Nevertheless capital is scarce in most developing countries, and there is a certain disenchantment with foreign consultancy services at the pre-feasibility and planning stages. Too many studies have ended up on the shelves as silent witnesses to wasted funds. This may not be the fault of the consultant, but it constitutes a serious problem which must be addressed.

The costs of foreign consultancy services have gone up considerably over the past few years but probably no more than the general rate of inflation. It is therefore not surprising that developing countries prefer to give orders to domestic consultants and have begun to realize the importance of stimulating the growth of a competent corps of local consultants.

It is doubtful whether costs can be kept down by competition. Competitive bidding involves the preparation of proposals and may add as much as 5% to the turnover of many firms. Invitations to bid should be limited to a short list of candidates. A method which might be worth trying is to start with a shortlist of say three consultants established on the basis of some process of pre-qualification. The three consultants would be invited to a joint meeting with the client to agree on the conditions of contract and the terms of reference; each would then submit his proposal. The consultants would be satisfied that the client knows in detail what he wants and the consultants would all be tendering equivalent information.

Choosing the lowest price is no guarantee of obtaining the best value for money. It is often argued that the best way to choose a consultant is to invite uncosted proposals from firms chosen on the basis of reputation, to rank the proposals in order of technical merit, and then to negotiate the price with the consultant who submitted the best proposal, although this procedure has the drawback of excluding new entrants.

Even this advice is not always easy to follow, since the client's key to success is both to choose the list of bidders well and to arrive at an adequate content for a proper price. Few developing countries are capable of doing this, and they therefore tend to be in the hands of their advisers to whom the consultants themselves often belong.

Generally speaking, costs will be reduced if consultants are brought in early, especially economists and management consultants. It is often advisable for the client to choose a consultant on the basis of reputation and involve him in the drafting of the terms of reference for each aspect of the set of problems to be solved. Once a first rate consultant has been chosen, arrangements can be made for contracts and sub-contracts.

## A. Ways to reduce costs

One way to reduce costs is to arrange for training of nationals from the developing countries. They can either be sent to the home office of foreign consultants or can be trained on the spot by consultancy firms hired on a long-term basis to help formulate and execute national and/or sectoral plans. This has worked well, since the long-term consultant has had time to become thoroughly acquainted with local conditions and the specific needs of the host country. He can also help select other consultants for specific projects.

The biggest saving can come from the way the client administers consultancy contracts, for delays are expensive. Much remains to be done at the local level to improve matters. Since some foreign consultants who are well established may try to retain their advantages, developing countries would be well advised to seek technical assistance in the use of consultants, especially so long as aid is tied.

Clients are now exercising their right to be involved in what the consultant is doing for them, which is also a good way for them to learn. However, they should clearly understand the consultant's role if they hope to establish good working relations, another important factor in eliminating waste and reducing costs.

A great deal of consultants' time is also wasted when contracts are being drawn up. In the developed countries standard contracts are in wide use, but the developing countries are often reluctant to use such contracts since they were not directly involved in the drafting. It would be a major step forward if internationally accepted contracts could be drawn up after consultation with the interested parties.

## B. Structure and Determinants of Fees

The most common methods of pricing consultancy services are the lump-sum fee, the fixed fee per man-months, and the fee related to the cost of construction (or other work).

The lump-sum fee is most easily set for certain standardised tasks, such as detailed design and preparation of specifications. The difficulty of defining cost levels, even for comparatively short periods of time, is now so great that many consultants refrain from committing themselves to a definite price.

The fee per man-month covers the salary of the persons assigned to the job, plus overhead and social charges, contingencies, interest and profit. The only drawback is that this does not incite the consultant to work as efficiently as possible. It is therefore fairly normal practice to define a cost ceiling for the assignment in order to assure the client that unreasonable delays will be avoided. It does not offer any guarantee, however, that the work will be finished, and the consultant may ask for renegotiation if he finds that he cannot keep to the original agreement, especially if he can show that delays were beyond his control.

A fee related to construction costs means that the more expensive the project, the more money the consultant makes. The method is therefore applied only in cases where standard solutions are possible and costs are known.

The cost of consulting services has increased rapidly during the pas few years, but it must be remembered that the consultant fee represents a very small part of the total investment. The most important objective for the client, also with reference to cost, remains the improvement of domestic capacity, including administration and collaboration with foreign consultants.

VI. Local Administration of Consultants

Poor administration is bound to increase the cost of consultants. Foreign consultants welcome clear-cut relations with local administrators but often find that no one is completely in charge. At present ministries and agencies tend to handle their own consultants but rarely supervise them. This state of affairs is unsatisfactory for several reasons: it can be uneconomical; it does not guarantee the desired transfer of knowledge; and it fails to achieve integrated planning and coordinated implementation.

Ideally, foreign and domestic consultants should be centrally administered. In many Latin-American countries this is done, as we mentioned earlier, through autonomous pre-investment funds. There are great potential advantages to this sort of central administration: waste can be reduced; learning and training can be increased; coordination can be improved; available capacity and skills can be inventoried; cost comparisons can be facilitated; and supervision and monitoring can provide a file of performance data. A consultancy unit in the central administration could be partially staffed by foreign experts.

In smaller countries at an early stage of development, efficient administration of consultants would facilitate an integrated approach to development and a balanced allocation of resources.

Developing countries often face serious problems of inconsistency, both horizontal and vertical. Consultants working in different regions or professional fields are rarely aware of each other's activities simply because they have not been instructed to keep in touch. Then, too, departments and agencies involved in different phases of macro- or micro-planning often fail to coordinate.

Central management of pre-investment studies could bring decided improvements. For example, construction and manufacturing firms often provide feasibility studies free of charge as a prelude to negotiations. Countries that accept such offers often find it diffi- cult to evaluate these reports, forgetting that they could call upon an independent consultant for a reasonable fee to get an appraisal. Central administration can also offer some guarantee that the wrong technology will not be bought, a fairly common and extremely expen- sive mistake.

A. Follow-up

Why do a large number of consultant studies end up on a shelf? It seems reasonable to assume that in many cases the problem is an administrative one. By the time a report has been printed, the con- sultant has left the country; and though a number of copies is dis- tributed to the government, no arrangements for follow-up have been made.

Follow-up should be decided upon when the terms of reference are being drafted. In that way the consultant will be available to ex- plain his analysis in detail and the reasons for his conclusions and recommendations.

Some bilateral development agencies have begun to provide consultancy firms with financing so that they will present the report to the government and discuss its implications. During these discussions, the possibility of extended collaboration in line with the consul- tant's recommendations is often evoked. Ideally representatives of other bilateral and multilateral agencies should also be invited to discuss the consultant's report.

B. Evaluation of Consultants

The importance of ex-post evaluation of development projects is being increasingly recognised. Many international agencies have made arrangements for such evaluation, although the results presented can create internal friction in the agency, and evaluation may be a source of embarrassment for the parties concerned, including the host government. Therefore evaluation of consultants' work must be planned for carefully from the beginning and included in the terms of reference.

Engineering consultants who are not interested in, or impressed by, the value of cost-benefit ratios or rates of return may consider it sufficient to show that their assignment was carried out efficiently, in time, and at the estimated costs. In other words, they find some form of cost effectiveness to be an adequate criterion. Management and economic consultants are more likely to be interested in actual rates of financial and economic return, since to them this seems to be the professional way to judge whether the expected results were in fact achieved.

Ex-post evaluation of projects may be done with varying degrees of attention to detail. Essentially what is of interest is to identify the actual costs and benefits and to compare them with the estimates made during the planning stage. Explaining the differences might entail a substantial amount of history-writing, which would probably be justified only exceptionally. It does not seem likely that demanding arrangements for monitoring, as part of a system of built-in evaluation, will be accepted by the developing countries in the near future, although forms of sophisticated evaluation will continue to be enforced by certain external agencies.

If one accepts that foreign and domestic consultants contribute significantly to the success of the planning and implementation of individual projects, there seems to be a strong case for a detailed study of the actual function of the principal consulting firm during the whole process of the consultant contract. If there is justification for monitoring and supervising the planning and implementation of individual projects, it would be equally logical to have built-in evaluation of the role played by consultants as well. The result could prove enlightening and could help the client make better use of consultant services. Though this might seem like an imposition, many consulting firms and especially those with a distinguished record, might welcome such evaluation, since it would produce information which the consulting firm has neither the mandate nor the inclination to provide. In other words, the evaluation of a specific consulting assignment could throw light on major constraints and thereby enable the client to take relevant action.

## VII. Guidelines and Rules of Development Lenders

The guidelines of the World Bank and the regional development banks for the use of consultants are similar:

They engage consultants for their own studies, for technical assistance, and for services contracted by their own borrowers;

The borrower is responsible for the selection of its own consultants, but may obtain guidance from the lender;

The consulting firm chosen must be approved by the lender (the IDB and World Bank also reserve the right to approve terms of reference and price);

The Banks make available their own information on consultants but abstain from making specific recommendations;

Preference is given by the banks to domestic consultants, when these are competitive, and to consortia of local and foreign firms;

Foreign consultants are free to choose the domestic consultant with whom they wish to collaborate.

The preference for domestic consultants raises the question of qualifications and cost. The fact that cost is secondary to quality might disqualify many local consultants. This is dealt with by lenders in their official documents in slightly different ways. The Asian Development Bank merely states that "other things being equal, preference will be given to domestic consultants or combinations of a consulting firm from a developed member country with consultants from a developing member country". The African Development Bank specifies that the firm must be "of acknowledged worldwide repute in the appraisal, construction, engineering and economic aspects of major projects comparable to the one at hand", as well as "experienced in the utilisation of local labour and resources and familiar with the prevailing conditions in developing countries". Here, domestic consulting firms would be disqualified on the basis of the first stipulation, while a good many, but not all, foreign consulting firms would be disqualified by the second stipulation.

The Inter-American Development Bank deals with the matter in relation to the cost of services. Although cost competition is discouraged, the Bank points out that "the economic development needs of its members require that the cost of services provided be maintained at reasonable and minimum levels consistent with acquisition of the technically qualified and competent services required. To this end, the Bank is prepared to render assistance to borrowers and beneficiaries in their contract negotiations..." More specifically, IDB may from time to time "provide technical cooperation in the training of contract negotiating officers and consulting services contract administrators of borrowers and beneficiaries". The IDB is also "prepared to designate an observer who shall serve only in an advisory capacity, to assist in the review of consulting firms' proposals, and attend meetings at which the borrower and beneficiary interviews, selects or negotiates with professional services firms".

The World Bank goes into somewhat greater detail. The borrower "should focus primarily on each firm's current professional qualifications, its recent performance on similar assignments, its understanding of the particular assignment at hand and the staff it has available when the work is required". It points out that differences in these qualitative aspects can be significant and can bear on the "quality of design and the overall cost of the project for which the services are needed". It further points out that consultant fees "normally are a small part of the total investment for a project". When countries are required by law or by general administrative regulations to invite priced proposals for consulting services, this should be done in a separate envelope to be opened only after the decision based on quality has been made.

Selection procedures used by the lenders are usually recommended to the borrowers but are not enforced. The World Bank normally invites from three to five firms to submit proposals for a study.(The African Development Bank does not give a figure, the Asian Development Bank suggests from five to seven and the IDB from three to eight). Its selection procedures are summarized as follows:

1. A Selection Committee is formed, comprised of qualified Bank staff concerned with the project in question.

2. The Bank staff responsible for the study prepare draft Terms of Reference and a list of capable firms, taking into account the views of the government agencies involved and available date in the Bank's files.

3. The Committee considers, modifies if necessary, and approves the Terms of Reference and short list of firms.

4. The Committee's recommendation is sent to the government for comment and approval.

5. Government suggestions for improvements in the Terms of Reference and/or justified objections to the list of firms are considered, but the Committee resists increasing the number of firms.

6. After the government's agreement has been received, requests for proposals (without financial terms) are prepared and sent to the consultants on the agreed list.

7. Proposals are evaluated by the Bank staff on the basis of the firms' experience in similar projects and environment, proposed program of work and qualifications of staff to be assigned; the Bank staff ranks the proposals in order of merit.

8. The Committee meets to review the recommendation and reaches a decision on the final ranking of the firms.

9. The Bank then invites the firm tentatively selected for contract negotiations in the Bank's Washington office.

10. If the negotiation with the selected firm is unsuccessful, the firm next in rank is asked to come for negotiations.

The success of a consultant firm's work depends to a great extent on the collaboration received in the host country. For that reason the World Bank have defined the functions of the full-time staff they normally ask the borrowers and government agencies to assign as counterparts, as follows:

1. to provide liaison on substantive matters between the consultants and government agencies and to direct the consultants to all available sources of data;

2. to receive training in the field of the study, through day-to-day exposure to the work of specialists. (Training over and above this normal exposure is often desirable. In such cases a detailed programme and budget for training should be included in the consultants' contract, and procedures should be established for the careful selection of counterpart staff to be assigned primarily for training purposes);

3. to review and discuss with the consultants all findings and recommendations, before they are presented to the government in the form of a report.

It is emphasized that if clerical, administrative and technical services are also supplied in support of the consultant, then this will reduce the foreign currency cost. Such services should be under the control and direction of the consulting firm, but related staff have a different relationship with consultants than counterpart staff.

## VIII. The Consultancy Profession in Developing Countries

Comparatively little information is available on the consultancy profession in the developing countries. Latin-America is fairly well advanced, although there are great differences between individual countries. Some Asian countries, particularly India and Pakistan, have a large number of consultants. In Africa the consulting profession is comparatively new.

As in the more industrialised countries, the engineering consultancy profession is the first to emerge, followed much later by management consulting and other disciplines. In the near future considerable interest will most likely be shown in drawing up national inventories of domestic consultants as well as a relevant national policy. Such a policy should of course be congruent with national development policy; it seems likely that practical solutions can be found within any type of political system: for example, consulting firms can be successful either as private or public enterprises.

The consultancy profession does not start early in any country; rather it is a specialized service offered when development has reached a certain stage. Independent engineering consultants usually branch off from the construction and manufacturing industries when these are important enough to sustain a corps of professional consultants. It is not surprising then that domestic consultancy capacity in the developing countries must be supplemented from external sources, not only for advanced technology, for which they will continue to be dependent on external inputs, but for a whole range of standard technologies.

Even if the situation in most developing countries is not as yet conducive to the growth of a domestic crops of consultants, the insistence on sovereignty and self-direction will increasingly force the issue. Developing countries will see to it that they get a greater share of the consultancy market through legal and contractual arrangements and joint ventures.

Most international consultants and multilateral development agencies encourage, at least in principle, the development of local consultancy firms. Foreign consultants can benefit from working with them, but the problem is to find capable local firms with no conflicting vested interests.

One way in which foreign consultants can help develop local firms is to set up subsidiaries initially managed by expatriate staff, which are gradually taken over by local staff. This has been done successfully in a number of cases, with the parent company retaining a minority interest. India, for example, has taken this kind of initiative.

It is to the advantage of the developing country to have foreign consultants employ a maximum number of domestic staff for each consultancy contract. In countries where the consultancy profession is advanced, a local consultant may sub-contract to a foreign consulting firm the sectors which need external inputs.

A. Indonesia: A Case Study in Developing Domestic Capacity

The case of Indonesia is of special interest because of the combined efforts of the Dutch and Indonesian authorities to improve Indonesian consultancy capacity. Like many developing countries, Indonesia wants its corps of local consultants to be in a position to bid on projects financed by the international agencies, primarily the World Bank and the Asian Development Bank. A Dutch mission visited Indonesia in 1972 to evaluate an application for assistance to develop the consultancy profession. The mission confined itself largely to contacts with existing consultancy organisations: the Association of Management Consultants IKINDO, and the Association of Technical Consultants PKTP.

Their members - about 30 in IKINDO and 10 in PKTP - were qualified but lacked experience. Only a few had worked in joint ventures with foreign consultants, and as it takes at least five years to acquire the experience necessary to compete with foreign consultants, they felt that some way of accelerating the process should be found. The solution, they said, was to arrange for various forms of direct collaboration with foreign consultant firms. This meant that, for there to be a transfer of knowledge, foreign consultants had to be persuaded to use the local consultants not only for simple tasks but also for qualified work. They recognized that this would incur expenses which the foreign consultants could not be expected to cover.

A programme of cooperation was worked out and an agreement concluded between the Dutch and Indonesian Governments covering a trial period of 30 months and an initial Dutch financial contribution of 1 million guilders. The authorities for the development programme were the national planning agency of Indonesia (BAPPENAS) and the International Technical Assistance Department (DITH) of the Dutch Foreign Ministry. A Dutch and an Indonesian project manager were made responsible for day-to-day operations under the guidance of an Indonesian Steering Committee, consisting of some 16 members, and of a small Dutch Advisory Body, comprised of representatives of the Dutch associations of engineering and management consultants.

Programme activities were twofold: helping Indonesian firms participate in on-going studies and/or projects; and establishing inventory, registration and classification systems, and professional and financial standards.

Though no one thought that progress could be made overnight, getting the programme underway was more difficult than had been expected. Potential clients - Indonesian government agencies, banks and investors - wanted detailed information about domestic firms to know who could do what. On the other hand, the consultants wanted work but were reluctant to release this information for tax reasons and also for fear that they might be judged inadequate. When Dutch consultants accompanied local consultants to discuss work possibilities with clients, it became painfully clear that most of the qualified work was being done by foreign consultants. Though Indonesian banks had lists of local consultants, they were strictly confidential. The membership lists of the consultancy associations were also difficult to use since no standards had been set for joining.

Other difficulties stemmed from the way the project itself had been organized. It became apparent that joint management was not working well, and full responsibility was finally handed over to the Indonesian project manager. The Steering Committee's role was crucial but its contribution depended, among other things, on the financial commitment of the national planning agency which, during the period of the initial agreement, proved to be inadequate.

Moreover, the national development plan did not allow for easy identification of potential projects for which consultancy services would be needed. Capacity for project planning and implementation in individual ministries and agencies varied considerably, as did their experience and ability to use consultants. While the responsibility for the Consultancy Development Project was placed in the central planning agency, no government policy for the use of foreign and domestic consultants had been formulated. It was one of the merits of the project that it actualized this question. The importance of making an inventory of available domestic consultancy services was brought to the attention of individual ministries. But by the end of the first contractual period, only the Ministry of Transport and Communications had made an attempt to draw up its own list, which did not however specify the capabilities of each consultancy firm.

The Indonesian Consultancy Development Project made enough progress to justify extension of the agreement, and a number of lessons can be learned. A consultancy development project will most likely help domestic clients see the advantages of using local consultants and to make government agencies better aware of areas in which their services can be used. Guidelines will probably be produced on standard terms of engagement for studies, actual work, and consultancy fees. Establishment of inventories and professional classifications will depend on initiatives taken by existing consultant associations and the government. A government policy requiring individual ministries and agencies to make use of and promote the corps of domestic consultants can help, especially if they are also required to draw up inventories in their own field of competence. A cursory investigation can identify the projects to be done in various sectors and sub-sectors and determine how many local consultants are available to carry out the planned programme and which services would have to be purchased in foreign currency at considerably higher prices.

## IX. The Need for an International Information System

The saying goes that it takes a consultant to write a specification for consultancy and adjudicate on proposals. In the absence of a consistent system and appropriate guidelines for the selection of consultants, developing countries might do well to hire "consultants on consultants". Even when standard procedures have been introduced and the principle of the short-list method accepted, the difficulty in obtaining information on the quality and performance of different consultants remains. In view of the developing countries' need for information, it is indeed surprising that proposals have not been made for an agency to serve the international community.

The following are some of the types of information that an international agency could provide, through meetings and seminars, courses, professional advice and publications:

- guidance on how to find suitable consultants;
- profiles of various types of experts;
- standards elaborated by different trade associations;
- techniques to measure and assess project feasibility;
- descriptions of good and bad terms of reference;
- prices of typical consulting services;
- management tools for project execution;
- case studies that show why projects fail or succeed, with special attention to terms of reference, staffing and local logistic support.

Though this list is far from comprehensive, it covers a range of potential services, situations and related information. Experience shows that certain mistakes occur repeatedly, often at great cost. Once the reasons for these mistakes are understood, measures to avoid them can be taken.

# CHAPTER VII

## A SUMMING UP

### I. Project Analysis and External Forces

All nations depend to some extent on external inputs and are subject
to foreign influence, but the developing countries, because of the
weakness of their institutional and financial resources, are particularly vulnerable. They are generally poorly equipped to manage
and control the transfer of resources and techniques. External forces
are subject to their own constraints: commercial and financial interests tend to follow the dictates of the market; bilateral agencies
have their own governments, auditors and public opinion watching
over them; multilateral agencies are limited by political and financial dependence and by their own administrative structure.

Some external agencies continue to pay close attention to criteria
and techniques of project analysis. Their insistence upon analysis
of financial and economic returns, control and responsibility, as
well as a number of other factors such as regional balance, equity,
protection of the environment, employment generation, and participation of women and youth has placed enormous demands on domestic planning agencies and has undoubtedly brought improvements in domestic
systems of project planning. However, external methods have often
been too sophisticated for domestic planning capacity, a problem
compounded by the fact that a variety of techniques and criteria
are applied. For example, EEC governments, the World Bank, Japan
and Sweden all use quite different methods. There are differences
even within individual donor countries.

Consequently domestic criteria for projects and programmes continue
to be used alongside foreign criteria, with little interpenetration.
External criteria are accepted, but only grudgingly, the transfer
of knowledge is inadequate and domestic capacity grows very slowly.
While domestic authorities dislike their dependence and resent inter-
ference, external agencies continue to be bound by their own procedures and terms of reference. To break out of this dilemma, developing countries will have to build adequate institutions which alone
can increase their self-reliance.

But, it can be asked, why has the process of institution-building
proved so slow? One obvious answer is that to meet pressing problems,
many countries did what seemed realistic under the circumstances.
As far as project planning is concerned, a promising example of
effective institution-building is the pre-investment funds that

certain Latin American countries have set up. They have succeeded in establishing early coordination and integration of pre-investment studies, sound and consistent criteria and follow-up. Domestic capacity in some instances has been improved by offering assistance to local consultants and to scientific and technological research.

It is up to each country to define the institutional arrangements best suited to promote self-reliance. But before adequate solutions can be proposed, the realities of domestic politics must be understood and needs for external services defined. A strong central agency for pre-investment studies could make government processes more consistent and could beneficially influence resource allocations, but it would need backing at the highest level and the power of the purse.

Most developing countries will need assistance to design and build a central projects institution. This assistance could either be requested from bilateral and multilateral agencies or be purchased abroad. Ideally, concessionary funds should be available to recruit an international team of consultants and experts in the various disciplines, and an international body should exist to provide information and impartial advice to which domestic projects institutions could turn. We shall explore this last suggestion in discussing the need for a national projects system.

## II. Institutional Structure and Project Analysis

Although our method has been more "impressionistic" than scientific, we are now ready to sum up the answers to the questions raised in Chapter One. In answer to the question "To what extent have appraisal techniques been adopted in the developing countries?", we have shown that with the exception of one or two institutions, professional techniques are not as a rule used for project appraisal; an examination of project alternatives is rare. In some of the countries we reviewed, technical feasibility is the overriding concern, especially when the emphasis is on getting basic infrastructure into place. In countries with socialist goals there is greater emphasis on institutional structure and some institutions take on new functions: banks, for example, become agents of project planning and administration. In countries where efforts have been made to decentralise investment authority and responsibility, formal appraisal techniques appear to be less important than participation and the selection of the "correct" course of action and of "making things work".

However, the demands of external agencies for Western-type project analysis are considerable and must be met. We have presented some evidence to show that the outcome of most externally financed

projects with respect to appraisal is predetermined (question 2);
if aid is tied, a certain type of technology must often be used.
This determines project selection irrespective of the rate of return,
provided it is "satisfactory", and influences institutional development.

As far as the influence of project-selection methods on institutions
is concerned (question 3), our observations are supported by those
of Rondinelli.

> "In many cases developing countries simply attempt to beat the
> aid agencies at their own game, adopting dual systems of analysis,
> feasibility testing, appraisal and management, at times establish-
> ing autonomous authorities within their own governments to ope-
> rate externally financed projects. One system is used primarily
> to obtain foreign funds and to comply with external requirements,
> the other to administer internal activities in traditional fash-
> ion" (1).

We therefore suggest that much thought should be given by donors and
recipients to the problem of reintegrating existing systems of project selection and management.

We discussed the need for suitable forms of project analysis and
institutions in the "soft" sector of rural development. Here it is
particularly important that institutions encompass all aspects. The
integrated treatment of rural development is new and rapidly expanding, mainly as a consequence of external influence, and highlights
the need for "supreme" project institutions, at national as well as
local levels responsible for negotiating project funding and technology as well as appraisal and monitoring (question 4).

The effective use of foreign consultants, the development of a competent corps of domestic consultants and their integration into a
national project system (question 5) should be given high priority.
Consultants should be monitored more closely. They should not be
hired unless their reports will be studies and used. External consultants should be expected to hire local staff as part of their
terms of reference. We have shown the need for "consultants on
consultants".

We leave question 6 - the use of external assistance to strengthen
institutions - to the final section of this chapter. First we would
like to comment on the changing nature of development assistance,
and we refer to the work of SIDA.

III. Changes in Development Assistance: The Swedish Case

If one accepts that the essence of development is educating people and building effective institutions, today there is considerable over-capacity in the industrialised countries which could be used to great mutual advantage in the Third World. The accumulated resources in terms of various types of know-how are tremendous, and human ingenuity and good will represent a force which could be set in motion by financial aid. A happy medium between the cynicism of using aid to subsidise exports and excessive preoccupation with over-ambitious objectives could be found if the aid effort were extensively delegated to a number of key institutions which have played a significant role in the development of industrialised countries.

Building institutions is a way of providing for the requirements of tomorrow and would therefore promote medium-range planning, a much neglected priority. We recognise that a great number of problems in developing countries are urgent and require immediate attention, but if this is done at the expense of effective institution-building, the very basis of development will remain weak and dependence will continue. In other words, the priorities of recipients must be challenged and donors should provide aid not in forms tied directly to their own exports but to types of collaboration, primarily institutional, which will set in motion a process based on confidence in rewards in the medium and long term through less formalised procedures. The best way to accomplish this would be for aid agencies to delegate the implementation of aid while retaining responsibility for executive policy and planning. It is worth noting that SIDA has already delegated to a great extent both planning and implementation of its aid activities. For example, voluntary organisations are used extensively, and assistance in agriculture and rural development is given in close collaboration with the Swedish University of Agriculture, which has employed a large number of persons for the purpose.

A promising form of development cooperation is the so-called Sister Industries Programme in Tanzania, by which private enterpreneurs in Sweden collaborate with enterpreneurs in Tanzania, who are thus able to profit from Swedish experience and know-how in small-scale industry. The programme includes assistance inter alia in the form of a) a private Swedish enterprise which acts as broker for both Swedish and Tanzanian companies, and b) negotiation assistance through a private Swedish law firm, which acts primarily to protect the interests of the Tanzanian companies. We propose that such types of initiative be generalised.

Normative policy would remain the prerogative of the Government and Parliament, and translating this policy into action would be the aid agency's major challenge. It would have to retain responsibility for

country and regional analyses, monitoring and supervision, information, audit and evaluation.

There are a great many institutions, agencies and associations which
could become executing agencies of the national aid agency. Our purpose here is not to rate them according to their importance. One way
to begin would be to look at the major agents in the principal sectors of development cooperation: agriculture, forestry and fishing;
demography and health; industry and physical infrastructure; education and research. It would be equally justified to look at institutions related to fundamental development problems and prerequisites
(2).

Aid agencies occasionally use such agencies and institutions as consultants, but they have no opportunity to establish permanent relations so that they could help build similar institutions as and when
requested by the developing countries. Their action is based on specific terms of reference limited in time and scope; this is due to
the fact that the aid programme, in response to the requests of recipients, is composed of a great number of projects which are phased
out over a comparatively short period of time. Such a situation does
not make for creativity and sustained effort.

It could make a great difference if agencies, associations and institutions could use funds reserved for the purpose to apply their
experience and know-how in direct collaboration with their counterparts in developing countries. Today they perforce restrict themselves
to what is requested. Assistance today is designed by bureaucrats
with the help of hired professionals. It ought to be the other way
around: assistance should be conceived and designed by professionals
with the help of experts on development.

A few examples will suffice to make our point:
- The Swedish Patent Office is a gold mine of information on
  inventions and techniques, many of which might suit the needs
  of developing countries; this information could be made available free of charge or at a modest fee, since most of the
  patents have expired.
- The Institute of Meteorology and Hydrology could help collect
  and analyse data to facilitate the planning of water supplies,
  irrigation, energy, agriculture and human settlements. It took
  years of work to prepare the necessary legislation for Swedish
  hydroelectric power as well as to collect hydrological data
  for each power station. In the present energy crisis, such data
  are badly needed in most developing countries and could have
  been made available if related institutions had been allowed
  to cooperate.

- Aid projects must also take environmental aspects into account even though this can create friction; recipients rarely appreciate the resulting restrictions and obligations. This could be dealt with in a more constructive way if the Environmental Protection Board were allowed to offer its services in building equivalent domestic institutions in the developing countries.
- Associations of consultants could be of immense value in helping to create corps of domestic consultants. Swedish state enterprises have an abundance of competent managers who have become superfluous as the result of mergers and discontinued activities; their experience could profit many developing countries.

Needless to say, the decentralisation of aid will create problems that should not be underestimated. However, if the industrialised countries cannot solve them, can developing countries be expected to put their own houses in order?

Decentralised aid presents a number of advantages:

- it would promote a higher degree of professionalism, more inventiveness and sense of risk;
- donors would have a greater interest in and experience of development problems;
- normal relations based on mutual interest would be established more quickly;
- the work of aid agencies would be simplified;
- there would be closer contact with the resource base;
- follow-up on the use of resources transferred and the evaluation of their effects would be improved;
- the know-how transferred and absorbed would increase;

Decentralised aid also presents some disadvantages:

- conflicts of interest among executing agencies within the donor country and among various donor countries will arise;
- executing agencies would be taken away from their domestic duties;
- there will be increased diplomatic risks because of greater and less controlled "official" contacts.

It seems to us that the advantages by far outweigh the disadvantages and there are few other alternatives if the present difficulties of development aid are to be overcome.

To play its role, the aid agency would have to have sufficient financial resources and authority to instruct the executing agencies. SIDA already has the right to instruct Embassies in its areas of competence. Instead of overburdening staff with operating responsibilities, as is presently the case, the aid agency would have time to plan, supervise and evaluate policy. Separating policy and planning from implementation is a decisive advantage. True planning and policy-making need feed-back from operations, but the Swedish aid agency is now an important, and almost unique, national resource of accumulated experience of development problems, and this resource can best be used to instruct and monitor the executing agencies and to initiate and process new policy.

IV. The Need for a National Projects System

The need for an integrated projects system has often been expressed but, with few exceptions, institutions have stopped short of the goal; instead, partial solutions - a central office of project evaluation or development bank screening of loan applications - have been adopted. We shall not attempt here to define the structure of an ideal projects institution, since different conditions prevail in each country. We can, however, draw attention to a few essential characteristics of such a system.

- Staff should be trained in all relevant disciplines. Some arrangement should be made between staff and line so that staff in the central projects institution remains in touch with operational realities and operational staff has a broader perception of viability criteria.

- Team work is indispensible, since complex problems cannot be solved by one person. Working parties should be used rather than permanent organisational units.

- An institutional "memory" should be set up. Part of the staff should be used to collect studies and reports, from which they would extract the essentials. At present little is done to profit from past mistakes.

- Management of foreign and domestic consultants should be the most important function of the institution, for they do most of the actual work of project design. Management should concentrate on policy, and especially on general guidelines and terms of reference, since administration would be the responsibility of operating departments and agencies.

- Attention should also be paid to policy on the purchase of foreign technology and the development of domestic technology. This is closely related to the use of consultants and requires a research and development function, including proper funding arrangements for other parts of the national system (universities, agencies, enterprises, local pilot projects). There is much more to technology than production techniques; what is needed is an "unpackaging" of industrial projects so that they will be organically integrated on the local level.

- The national projects institution should be responsible for overall monitoring and supervision, including accounting and audit (ex-post evaluation). Though the institution itself would only supervise the administration of studies and the project cycle, it would ensure that there are sufficient bankable investment projects and that unnecessary studies are avoided.

- It should keep a close watch on mobilisation, decentralisation and organisation of activities at the local level.

- The institution should retain control over certain funds.

Admittedly, this is a very ambitious scheme, but there is still much to be done to prevent the waste of scarce resources and to reduce dependence on external interests. This dependence tends to perpetuate a double system of alien and domestic project planning and execution. Even in agriculture and rural development, projects are usually prepared by external staff. As the task of reducing dependence and improving domestic management of the project cycle is enormous, measures should be practical and confined to essentials; refined methods should be avoided, except when absolutely necessary.

Information and objective advice as well as evaluation of such information and advice are prerequisites for improved domestic capacity and reduced dependence. This problem is now by and large handled on a case by case basis to meet pressing needs. Though bilateral and multilateral donors provide support for the selection of consultants, procurement and negotiations, such assistance is still insufficient in relation to needs. We examined earlier the potential value of an international information system; ideally, such an organisation would provide essential information and advice on the project cycle and serve as a point of reference for the central projects institution at the national level. Its structure would reflect the requirements of the national institution.

These requirements are extensive, and the growth of both an international and a national institution would have to be carefully programmed. There is plenty of expertise available to advise on the design of such institutions, and recruiting professional staff for operational and advisory functions would not be difficult. The problem is to guarantee impartiality and freedom from ties, without which creative advice is impossible. This can probably only be done through careful selection of staff. Such an international organisation would probably have to be voluntary rather than intergovernmental.

An international centre for information and advice would not prejudge technology and cost, for countries have different needs and priorities, but it would provide a greater range of choice. Often

the requirements of scale and the cost of certain types of infrastructure, plant and installation are not clearly perceived, and
it might be possible to reduce the margin of error considerably.
This is especially true when a country wants to install a new type
of plant or when a few foreign firms dominate a particular technology. It may not be easy for an international organisation to collect
information on technology and costs, but the need is great enough
to justify the effort.

The main task of an aid agency would then be to assist in problem-
solving and to deliver resources efficiently. The aid agency would
be a small organisation concerned mainly with policy formulation
and guidelines for executive arms. It would be in close touch with
the domestic resource base. Decentralisation of the aid agency's
work could promote normalisation of donor-recipient relations thanks
to direct contact between departments, agencies, institutions and
corporations. Development cooperation would then become a reality
for a broader cross-section of the population.

There is a growing  trend towards decentralisation of aid. Aid
agencies already delegate much of the implementation of projects and
programmes and promote cooperation between institutions at home and
abroad. However, even more decentralisation is desirable. A national
projects system could bring added impetus to it.

FOOTNOTES

## CHAPTER I

1. Parts of this section are drawn from Baum, W.C., the World Bank Project Cycle, *Finance and Development*, 15,4, pp. 10-17, December 1978.

2. See, for example, Little, I.M.D. and Mirrlees J.A. *Manual of Industrial Project Analysis for Developing Countries; Vol II Social Cost-Benefit Analysis*, OECD Development Centre, Paris 1968; Scott, M.F.G., J.D. MacArthur and D.M.G. Newberry. *Project Appraisal in Practice*, Heinemann Educational Books, London 1976; Squire, L., & van der Tak, H.G., *Economic Analysis of Projects*, IBRD, Johns Hopkins University Press, Baltimore and London, 1975.

3. As quoted by J.D. MacArthur and G.A. Amin (eds), Cost-Benefit Analysis and Income Distribution in Developing Countries: A Symposium, *World Development* 6,2, 1978, p. 234.

4. For a strong "counter-view" of cost-benefit analysis, see Peter Self, *Econocrats and the Policy Process: The Politics and Philosophy of Cost-Benefit Analysis*, MacMillen, London, 1975.

5. Notably Albert Hirschman, *Development Projects Observed*, Brookings Institution, Washington D.C. 1967; John King, *Economic Development Projects and Their Appraisal: Cases and Principles from the Experience of the World Bank*, IBRD, Johns Hopkins Press, Baltimore 1967; Albert Waterston, *Development Planning: Lessons of Experience*, IBRD, Johns Hopkin Press, Baltimore, 1965, and Naomi Caiden and Aaron Wildavsky, *Planning and Budgeting in Poor Countries*, John Wiley, New York, 1974.

6. Wilson, F.A. Planning for Project Management, *J. Admin Overseas*, XVIII, 3, 202 - 208 (July 1979).

7. Imboden, N. *A Management Approach to Project Appraisal and Evaluation with Special Reference to Non-Directly Productive Projects*, Development Centre, OECD, Paris, 1978.

8. Rondonelli, D.A. International Assistance Policy and Development Project Administration: the impact of imperious rationality, *International Organisation*, 30, 4, (Autumn 1970) 573-605.

CHAPTER II

1. Little, I.M.D., and J.A. Mirrlees, Manual of Industrial Project Analysis in Developing Countries, Vol II, Social Cost-Benefit Analysis, Development Centre, OECD, Paris 1969.

2. Dasgupta, P.S., and S.A. Marglin, and A.K. Sen, Guidelines for Project Evaluation, United Nations, New York 1972.

3. Squire, L., and H.G. van der Tak, Economic Analysis of Projects, World Bank Research Publication, Washington D.C. 1975.

4. Ministry of Overseas Development, A Guide to the Economic Appraisal of Projects in Developing Countries, HMSO London, (revised edition) 1977.

5. USAID, Evaluation Handbook, Washington D.C. 1972.

6. Vaitsos, C.V., "Suggestions for possible UNDP action in the field of technological development in the Third World", mimeo.

7. A recent United Nations model of the world economy estimated that in order to reduce the gap between developed and developing countries by half by the year 2000, the developing countries would have to increase their GNP by 7% per year as the developed countries slow down theirs to 36% per year. This in turn would require that the developing countries invest 40% of their GNP and that agricultural development be drastically changed as well as the conditions mentioned above. (Closing the Rich-Poor Gap?)

8. It has been estimated that "without changes in present trends, transnational enterprises would control more than 40% of world production (excluding the centrally planned nations) before the end of the 1900s". RIO, Reshaping the International Order, New York: E.P. Dutton and Co. Inc., 1976.

9. Faber, M., and D. Seers (eds) The Crisis in Planning, Chatto & Windus, London, 1972, Vol. 1, p. 24.

10. Waterston, A., Development Planning: Lessons of Experience, Johns Hopkins Press, Baltimore 1965, p. 340.

11. Griffin, K., and J. Enos., Planning Development, Addison, London, 1972, pp. 203 - 204.

12. Joy L & G.B. Lamb, "Planning and the Political Process", Bellagio Working Party on Planning Models for Income Distribution and Employment, mimeo, April 1973.

13. Cibotti, R. and O.J. Bardeci, "A Critical Approach to Planning in Latin America". Report by Raul Prebisch to the Inter-American Development Bank, April 1970.

14. Little, I.M.D. and J.A. Mirrlees, Project Appraisal and Planning for Developing Countries, Heinemann Educational Books Ltd., London 1974, pp. 84-86.

15. Tinbergen has suggested that all planning functions be integrated in one single agency or department. See Tinbergen, J., Development Planning, 1967, Chapter 12.

16. Chambers, R., Managing Rural Development: Ideas and Experiences from East Africa, Scandinavian Institute of African Studies, Uppsala 1974, pp. 92-93.

17. Ibid p. 94.

18. Hirschman, A.D., Development Projects Observed, Brookings Institution, Washington, D.C., 1967, p. 35.

19. Ibid p. 13.

20. Birgegard, L.E., The Project Selection Process in Developing Countries, Economic Research Institute, Stockholm School of Economics, Stockholm, 1975, p. 201

21. Ibid p. 170.

22. Ibid p. 171.

23. The dominating sectors of World Bank lending until well into the 1960s were electric power and transportation. See Mason and Asher, The World Bank since Bretton Woods, Brookings Institution, Washington D.C., 1973, p. 258. The Bank is required by its articles to use "objective economic criteria", although it is also possible to maintain that the criteria employed for almost any type of project are economically objective as long as even modest efforts at quantification have been made.

24. Formal education in project analysis seems to be directly related to practical emphasis on national planning and work on pre-feasibility. In Colombia, for example, where national planning was an established routine and FONADE was in charge of much of the preinvestment studies, the Andes University worked on a practical textbook for the masters program in economics.

25. During the last 25 years more than 50 development banks have been financed by the World Bank for a total of over US $2 billion. See Diamond, W., Appraising Development Banks, Finance and Development, June 1974.

26. Gittinger, J.O., *Economic Analysis of Agricultural Projects*, Johns Hopkins Press, Baltimore, 1972, p.1.

27. One example of what is needed is project screening, which if implemented pays off handsomely but is a direct challenge to many vested interests. It is therefore an institutional challenge which at the moment very few developing countries have met. Screening at the identification stage can only take the negative form of preventing the preparation of projects which for some reason are unlikely to succeed, or of changing project formulation so as to meet certain requirements. It does not in itself guarantee comparison between alternative approaches or solutions, unless work at the feasibility level has resulted in comparable alternatives. Several multilateral and bilateral agencies have screening systems that check all projects before approval against an extensive list of criteria. Developing countries will have to design their own systems with due consideration to such factors as the cost of early screening in terms of prefeasibility work on alternatives, staff or organisational requirements, and any negative influence on the rate of investment and execution.

CHAPTER III

1. Ministry of the Interior, *Incentives to Industry and Farming in North-east Brazil*, Recife, 1973.

2. Central Planning Office, Federal Ministry of Economic Development and Reconstruction, Federal Republic of Nigeria, *Second National Development Plan (1975-80)*, Lagos (no date).

3. Central Planning Office, Federal Ministry of Economic Development & Reconstruction, Federal Republic of Nigeria, *Guidelines for the Third National Development Plan 1975-80*, Lagos, (no date) p. 21.

4. Economic Planning Unit, Federal Republic of Nigeria, *Manual on Project Preparation for the National Reconstruction and Development Plan 1970-74*, Lagos (1969).

5. Ibid., p. 5.

6. Federal Ministry of Information, Federal Republic of Nigeria, *Second National Development Plan 1970-74*, Lagos (1970), p. 333.

7. Central Planning Office, Federal Ministry of Economic Development and Reconstruction, Federal Republic of Nigeria, *Third National Development Plan 1975/80, Submission of Projects and Programmes*, EPU 126/vol. II/627.

8. Ibid., p. 5.

9. Ministry of Trade and Industry, State Government of Kano, *Industrialisation of Kano State; A Guide for Investors*, May 1972, p. 35.

10. Comite de Asesoramiento de la Presidencia de la Republica (COAD) eds, La Revolucion Nacional Peruana, Lima, Peru, 1972.

11. Oficina Sectorial de Planificacion, Ministero de Industria y Comerciao, Sistema Sectorial de Pre-Inversion, Documento de Trabajo, Diciembre 1973.

12. Schneider, Hartmut, National Objectives and Project Appraisal in Developing Countries, OECD Development Centre Study, Paris 1975, p. 89 and pp. 93-95.

13. Instituto Nacional de Planificacion, Normas para elaborar estudios de proyectos industriales, Lima 1973.

14. Rweyemamu, J., Underdevelopment and Industrialisation in Tanzania: A Study of Perverse Capitalist Industrial Development, Oxford University Press, London 1973, pp. 195-198.

15. Rweyemamu, J., op. cit., pp. 195-198.

16. The others are the State Mining Corporation, the Small Industries Development Organisation (largely concerned with promotion), the National Textile Corporation, the Board of Internal Trade and the State Motor Company.

17. Tanzania Rural Development Bank, A Manual of Operational Policies and Procedures, Dar es Salaam, May 1972.

18. Ibid., p. 18.

19. About 80% of capital investments and of revenues of State economic enterprises refer to the sectors of transportation, fuel supply and public utilities.

## CHAPTER IV

1. For an account of the self interest of donors see Mande, T., From Aid to Recolonisation. Lessons of a Failure, Harrap, London, 1973.

2. Foreign and Commonwealth Office, Overseas Development Administration, A Guide to Project Appraisal in Developing Countries, London, 1977.

3. The distinction between "productive" and "non-productive" projects is invidious and should be avoided.

4. World Bank, The World Bank Group: Policies and Operations, September 1974, p. 45.

5.  IBRD, Annual Report FY 1973.

6.  Mason E.S. & R.E. Asher, The World Bank Since Bretton Woods, The Brookings Institution, Washington D.C. 1973.

7.  Ibid., p. 592.

8.  Ibid., p. 751.

9.  Ibid., p. 567.


CHAPTER V

1.  Lele, Uma, The Design of Rural Development, Lessons from Africa, World Bank/Johns Hopkins University Press, Baltimore 1975, p. 20.

2.  Ibid., p. 20.

3.  See MacArthur J.D. and G.A. Amin, Cost Benefit Analysis and Income Distribution in Developing Countries: A Symposium, World Development 6,2, February 1978, p. 234.

4.  See Birgegard, L.E., The Project Selection Process in Developing Countries. Economic Research Institute, Stockholm, 1975, pp. 49-50.

5.  Baum, W.C. The World Bank Project Cycle, Finance & Development, 15, 4 December 1978, p. 12.

6.  Israel, Arturo, Toward Better Project Implementation, Finance & Development 15, 1 March 1978, pp. 27-30.

7.  Chambers, R., Project Selection for Poverty-Focussed Rural Development: Simple is Optimal, in Cost-Benefit Analysis and Income Distribution in Developing Countries: A Symposium, World Development 6, 2 February 1978 pp. 209-225.

8.  Chambers, op. cit. p. 211.

9.  Chambers, R., Managing Rural Development: Ideas and Experiences from East Africa, Scandinavian Institute of African Studies, Uppsala, 1974.

10. Imboden, N., A Management Approach to Project Appraisal and Evaluation with Special Reference to Non-Directly Productive Projects, Development Centre, OECD, Paris 1978.

11. Kulp, E.M. Rural Development Planning: Systems Analysis and Working Method, Praeger Special Studies in International Economics and Development, New York 1970.

12.   Kulp, E.M., op.cit. pp. 296 - 299.

13.   Kulp, E.M., op. cit. p. 318.

14.   Kulp, E.M. op.cit. p. 51.

15.   Chambers op.cit. p. 43.

16.   Chambers op.cit. p. 53.

17.   Chambers op.cit. p. 44.

18.   Imboden op.cit. pp. 20 - 21.

19.   Imboden op.cit. p. 105.

20.   Heimpel, C., Project Idea, Planning and Implementation:
      Some suggestions for a new approach to the planning of
      agricultural development projects. Economics, Vol. 16,
      (no date) pp. 106-107.


CHAPTER VII

1.    Rondinelli, op. cit., p. 597.

2.    The following types of potential executing agencies will
      suffice as an illustration:  the national audit agency; the
      national bureau of statistics; the state agency for adminis-
      trative development; the environmental protection board;
      the energy planning agencies; the national patent office;
      the national forest service; the national board of industries;
      the state enterprises corporation; the national bureau of
      standards; the national association of engineering industries;
      the national association of insurance companies; the national
      associations of consultants.

# OECD SALES AGENTS
## DÉPOSITAIRES DES PUBLICATIONS DE L'OCDE

ARGENTINA - ARGENTINE
Carlos Hirsch S.R.L., Florida 165, 4° Piso (Galería Guemes)
333 BUENOS AIRES, Tel. 33.1787.2391 y 30.7122

AUSTRALIA - AUSTRALIE
Australia and New Zealand Book Company Pty, Ltd.,
10 Aquatic Drive, Frenchs Forest, N.S.W. 2086
P.O. Box 459, BROOKVALE, N.S.W. 2100

AUSTRIA - AUTRICHE
OECD Publications and Information Center
4 Simrockstrasse 5300 BONN. Tel. (0228) 21.60.45
Local Agent/Agent local :
Gerold and Co., Graben 31, WIEN 1. Tel. 52.22.35

BELGIUM - BELGIQUE
CLS
35, avenue de Stalingrad, 1000 BRUXELLES. Tel. 02.512.89.74

BRAZIL - BRÉSIL
Mestre Jou S.A., Rua Guaipa 518,
Caixa Postal 24090, 05089 SAO PAULO 10. Tel. 261.1920
Rua Senador Dantas 19 s/205-6, RIO DE JANEIRO GB.
Tel. 232.07.32

CANADA
Renouf Publishing Company Limited,
2182 St. Catherine Street West,
MONTRÉAL, Quebec H3H 1M7. Tel. (514)937.3519
522 West Hasting,
VANCOUVER, B.C. V6B 1L6. Tel. (604) 687.3320

DENMARK - DANEMARK
Munksgaard Export and Subscription Service
35, Nørre Søgade
DK 1370 KØBENHAVN K. Tel. +45.1.12.85.70

FINLAND - FINLANDE
Akateeminen Kirjakauppa
Keskuskatu 1, 00100 HELSINKI 10. Tel. 65.11.22

FRANCE
Bureau des Publications de l'OCDE,
2 rue André-Pascal, 75775 PARIS CEDEX 16. Tel. (1) 524.81.67
Principal correspondant :
13602 AIX-EN-PROVENCE : Librairie de l'Université.
Tel. 26.18.08

GERMANY - ALLEMAGNE
OECD Publications and Information Center
4 Simrockstrasse 5300 BONN Tel. (0228) 21.60.45

GREECE - GRÈCE
Librairie Kauffmann, 28 rue du Stade,
ATHÈNES 132. Tel. 322.21.60

HONG-KONG
Government Information Services,
Sales and Publications Office, Baskerville House, 2nd floor,
13 Duddell Street, Central. Tel. 5.214375

ICELAND - ISLANDE
Snaebjörn Jönsson and Co., h.f.,
Hafnarstraeti 4 and 9, P.O.B. 1131, REYKJAVIK.
Tel. 13133/14281/11936

INDIA - INDE
Oxford Book and Stationery Co. :
NEW DELHI, Scindia House. Tel. 45896
CALCUTTA, 17 Park Street. Tel. 240832

INDONESIA - INDONÉSIE
PDIN-LIPI, P.O. Box 3065/JKT., JAKARTA, Tel. 583467

IRELAND - IRLANDE
TDC Publishers - Library Suppliers
12 North Frederick Street, DUBLIN 1 Tel. 744835-749677

ITALY - ITALIE
Libreria Commissionaria Sansoni :
Via Lamarmora 45, 50121 FIRENZE. Tel. 579751
Via Bartolini 29, 20155 MILANO. Tel. 365083
Sub-depositari:
Editrice e Libreria Herder,
Piazza Montecitorio 120, 00 186 ROMA. Tel. 6794628
Libreria Hoepli, Via Hoepli 5, 20121 MILANO. Tel. 865446
Libreria Lattes, Via Garibaldi 3, 10122 TORINO. Tel. 519274
La diffusione delle edizioni OCSE è inoltre assicurata dalle migliori
librerie nelle città più importanti.

JAPAN - JAPON
OECD Publications and Information Center,
Landic Akasaka Bldg., 2-3-4 Akasaka,
Minato-ku, TOKYO 107 Tel. 586.2016

KOREA - CORÉE
Pan Korea Book Corporation,
P.O. Box n° 101 Kwangwhamun, SÉOUL. Tel. 72.7369

LEBANON - LIBAN
Documenta Scientifica/Redico,
Edison Building, Bliss Street, P.O. Box 5641, BEIRUT.
Tel. 354429 - 344425

MALAYSIA - MALAISIE
and/et SINGAPORE - SINGAPOUR
University of Malaysia Co-operative Bookshop Ltd.
P.O. Box 1127, Jalan Pantai Baru
KUALA LUMPUR. Tel. 51425, 54058, 54361

THE NETHERLANDS - PAYS-BAS
Staatsuitgeverij
Verzendboekhandel Chr. Plantijnnstraat
S-GRAVENAGE. Tel. nr. 070.789911
Voor bestellingen: Tel. 070.789208

NEW ZEALAND - NOUVELLE-ZÉLANDE
Publications Section,
Government Printing Office,
WELLINGTON: Walter Street. Tel. 847.679
Mulgrave Street, Private Bag. Tel. 737.320
World Trade Building, Cubacade, Cuba Street. Tel. 849.572
AUCKLAND: Hannaford Burton Building,
Rutland Street, Private Bag. Tel. 32.919
CHRISTCHURCH: 159 Hereford Street, Private Bag. Tel. 797.142
HAMILTON: Alexandra Street, P.O. Box 857. Tel. 80.103
DUNEDIN: T & G Building, Princes Street, P.O. Box 1104.
Tel. 778.294

NORWAY - NORVÈGE
J.G. TANUM A/S Karl Johansgate 43
P.O. Box 1177 Sentrum OSLO 1. Tel. (02) 80.12.60

PAKISTAN
Mirza Book Agency, 65 Shahrah Quaid-E-Azam, LAHORE 3.
Tel. 66839

PHILIPPINES
National Book Store, Inc.
Library Services Division, P.O. Box 1934, MANILA.
Tel. Nos. 49.43.06 to 09, 40.53.45, 49.45.12

PORTUGAL
Livraria Portugal, Rua do Carmo 70-74,
1117 LISBOA CODEX. Tel. 360582/3

SPAIN - ESPAGNE
Mundi-Prensa Libros, S.A.
Castello 37, Apartado 1223, MADRID-1. Tel. 275.46.55
Libreria Bastinos, Pelayo 52, BARCELONA 1. Tel. 222.06.00

SWEDEN - SUÈDE
AB CE Fritzes Kungl Hovbokhandel,
Box 16 356, S 103 27 STH, Regeringsgatan 12,
DS STOCKHOLM. Tel. 08/23.89.00

SWITZERLAND - SUISSE
OECD Publications and Information Center
4 Simrockstrasse 5300 BONN. Tel. (0228) 21.60.45
Local Agents/Agents locaux
Librairie Payot, 6 rue Grenus, 1211 GENÈVE 11. Tel. 022.31.89.50
Freihofer A.G., Weinbergstr. 109, CH-8006 ZÜRICH.
Tel. 01.3634282

TAIWAN - FORMOSE
National Book Company,
84-5 Sing Sung South Rd, Sec. 3, TAIPEI 107. Tel. 321.0698

THAILAND - THAILANDE
Suksit Siam Co., Ltd., 1715 Rama IV Rd,
Samyan, BANGKOK 5. Tel. 2511630

UNITED KINGDOM - ROYAUME-UNI
H.M. Stationery Office, P.O.B. 569,
LONDON SE1    9NH. Tel. 01.928.6977, Ext. 410 or
49 High Holborn, LONDON WC1V 6 HB (personal callers)
Branches at: EDINBURGH, BIRMINGHAM, BRISTOL,
MANCHESTER, CARDIFF, BELFAST.

UNITED STATES OF AMERICA - ÉTATS-UNIS
OECD Publications and Information Center, Suite 1207,
1750 Pennsylvania Ave., N.W. WASHINGTON D.C.20006.
Tel. (202) 724.1857

VENEZUELA
Libreria del Este, Avda. F. Miranda 52, Edificio Galipan,
CARACAS 106. Tel. 32.23.01/33.26.04/33.24.73

YUGOSLAVIA - YOUGOSLAVIE
Jugoslovenska Knjiga, Terazije 27, P.O.B. 36, BEOGRAD.
Tel. 621.992

Les commandes provenant de pays où l'OCDE n'a pas encore désigné de dépositaire peuvent être adressées à :
OCDE, Bureau des Publications, 2, rue André-Pascal, 75775 PARIS CEDEX 16.

Orders and inquiries from countries where sales agents have not yet been appointed may be sent to:
OECD, Publications Office, 2 rue André-Pascal, 75775 PARIS CEDEX 16.